SHATTERED BUT SHELTERED

The Aftermath of Childhood Sexual Assault

Karen A. Smart, Ph.D.

TABLE OF CONTENTS

PREFACE

This book is dedicated to survivors of sexual assault, but especially to those who were minors when the assault took place. Part One is the true story of Martha's encounter with childhood sexual assault and the consequences that followed. The names have been changed to protect the identities of the parties involved. The concept for this book grew out of a desire to give hope to others who have had a similar experience, and to help survivors of sexual assault develop a spirit of resilience in the face of adversity. Part Two is a research based account of the fallout from sexual assault, with examples of how Martha's experiences support pieces of the research. This is followed by practical ways to avoid self-destruction in the aftermath. Since the research is centered around Martha's experience, many of the cases are from the perspective of females. However, this is not to discount that males can be similarly affected. This can be a conversation starter for clinicians, therapists and youth leaders who facilitate support groups for victims of sexual assault. It can also be used as a springboard for addressing high school students who are about to leave home for college, as well as college students living on campus who find themselves away from home for the first time. There are theoretical limitations to the research component, as the researcher's experience is the lens through which the literature was examined. Nevertheless, the content of this book can have a major influence on the way survivors of sexual assault handle these adverse circumstances, and significantly impact their quality of life going forward.

Acknowledgments

I would like to thank God for the perseverance to complete this project. I would also like to thank my close friend and colleague, Dr. Natalie March for the countless hours of proofreading and content editing. Many thanks to my sister, Dr. Cameale Smart, and to Licensed Clinical Social Worker, Pastor Alphod Sinclair for your valuable feedback. I would also like to thank my family for your understanding, as I spent numerous hours in seclusion during the writing process. Finally, to my close friends, I would like to express special appreciation for your generosity in supporting this project.

PROLOGUE

The stench of the gutters made Martha's stomach turn as she and her sister, Eve peeked out from the back seat of the 1969 Hillman Minx. As they made their way through the narrow streets near Grandma Sutton's house, Uncle Jim steered the white Hillman slowly and carefully through the crowds of people who barely moved a muscle, as if in no real hurry to get out of the way. The stray dogs wandering around seemed to be aware enough to scurry off to the side of the road as the vehicle passed by; but the people remained in their positions, apparently comfortable with the filth around them. Young men perched on sidewalks, while scantily dressed girls sat on low benches on the side of the road, leaving little room for cars. Young girls who seemed barely old enough to have children were seen carrying their babies on their hips, as if it were a badge of honor. Some were barefooted, and others dragged their feet in shabby-looking slippers, shouting greetings to their friends and neighbors as they walked up and down the streets with no specific destination. Garbage littered the streets and dogs left their waste in indiscriminate places, where cars and people alike trod through it and spread it around. Martha wondered why this did not seem to bother anyone else around her. "I can't stand the smell," whispered Martha to her sister. "Me neither," said Eve. "But mom will be back before you know it." Tears welled up in Martha's eyes and she squeezed her eyes shut to prevent them from spilling over.

Grandma Sutton's house was not so bad when they spent summers there; but now they were moving to Baker's Town to live with their paternal grandmother – at least until their mother could come back from America and take them to live with her like she promised. The realization that this would be their home for an indefinite time filled Martha with an overwhelming sense of sadness. She remembered the first time that she had spent the summer at Grandma Sutton's home a few years back. She had screamed bloody murder when they put her in bed and turned off the lights that first night. "I want to go to grandma's room!" she had screamed. The dark scared her tremendously. There was always a lamp burning in Grandma Martin's one-room house where she had lived with her mom, her older brother, Grayson, and her two sisters, Eve and Connie. Grandma Martin had no electricity, so they used a kerosine lamp which they turned down low when it was bedtime. For the first nine years of her life this was all she knew. But at Grandma Sutton's, the room was entirely dark at bedtime and Martha was terrified.

She had gotten used to the dark after that first summer, but she could not get used to the filth on the streets. She felt a compulsive need to spit when she saw the piles of animal feces. She wanted to puke when she smelled the garbage which were in piles on every corner, waiting for the garbage truck which seemed to come very infrequently. Some of the residents took it upon themselves to sweep the gutters sometimes and push the waste down into the manholes on the corner of the streets, which she assumed accounted for the smell that pervaded their surroundings.

The Sutton family was one of the few families in the community that owned a car. They had been residents of the community for years, and they were well known and highly respected among their neighbors. Uncle Jim waved occasionally as the young men shouted greetings. When they pulled up in front of the big iron gate, Uncle Jim got out and opened the lock. He placed planks on the sidewalk so he could drive up off the road into the paved yard, then he locked the big green gate behind him. As the lock clicked into place, Martha felt a sense of finality.

This time Martha found it difficult to fully appreciate the beauty of Grandma Sutton's home. She barely noticed the fresh coating of paint that Grandpa Sutton had put on the exterior walls since she was there last; or the new shelves that he had installed next to the kitchen window. She barely heard the beautiful green and white parrot when he greeted them with the familiar chant, "Pretty Paul...pretty, pretty, pretty Paul" in a sing-song voice. Grandma Sutton greeted them with a brisk nod. "This is where the two of you will sleep," she said. "You can place your clothes into these drawers." As they put away their meager belongings, Martha said to Eve, "How long do you think it will take mommy to come back for us?" "I don't know," replied Eve, "But I hope it will be soon."

PART ONE
MARTHA'S STORY

Chapter 1

WHERE IT ALL BEGAN

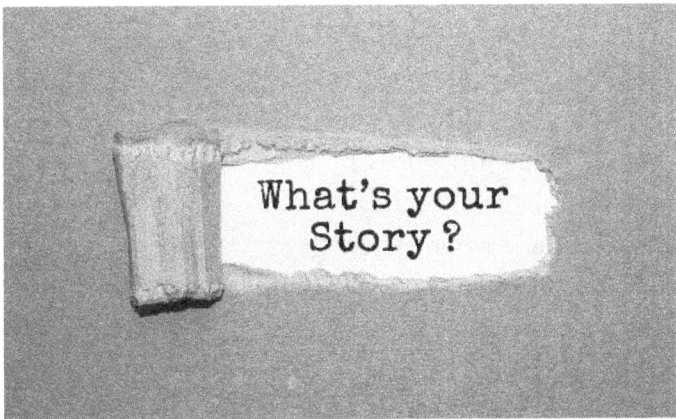

What's your Story?

IT WAS ANOTHER dreary Monday morning in Montvale, Jamaica, and 10-year-old Martha felt anxious as she got ready for school. Her stomach growled as she put on her green skirt and white blouse. Her uniform was not like the other children's. Martha's grandmother had made this skirt especially for her because there was simply not enough material to make the tunic which represented the proper uniform. She put on the brown, high-heeled church shoes that she was now wearing to school because her grandmother could not afford the proper shoes. It was time to go. *I guess there is nothing to eat this morning,* she thought to herself. Martha sipped her tea made from soursop leaves. She could barely taste the sugar, as there was only a little bit left in the crumpled, brown paper bag she found on the wooden table in the kitchen.

As Martha climbed through the barbed wire fence at the back of the yard to walk over to Payton Hall School, the school bell chimed. That was the early bell, Martha figured, and in her hurry to get there before the late bell rang, she fell against the wire and ripped the tender skin in the palm of her left hand. With tears rolling down her cheeks and blood dripping from her palm, she ran back to the house.

Grandma Martin rushed out of the house to meet her. "What is this commotion all about?" She asked. "I fell and cut my hand!" cried Martha. Grandma Martin patiently bandaged the wound with strips of white cloth. "You will have to stay home today," she said. Martha was relieved; she was too hungry anyway, and she did not feel like going to school to be ridiculed by teachers and students alike about her 'special' uniform.

I wish Eve were here, Martha thought to herself. Martha missed Eve. This was the first time she and her older sister were ever separated. She felt closer to Eve than to her other siblings, as she and Eve were the only two who had the same father. They were only 11 months apart in age and she often felt like they were twins. They dressed alike, did everything together, and never fought. They even finished each other's sentences at times. Martha's brother, Grayson was only three years older than Eve. Martha knew Grayson's father lived nearby, but she had never met him. Connie was three years younger than Martha, and she also had a different father. Martha had met Connie's father only once. Connie was only a baby when he came over to take the whole family to the beach. That was a fun day Martha recalled; but that was the last day she ever saw him.

Martha felt a bit lonely as she meandered around the yard, nursing her wounded hand. She thought about the exchange she had with her fourth-grade teacher the Friday before. "I am not going to waste my time trying to get you caught up on long division," Ms. Sampson had told her. "You have missed too much time in school, and you will not pass the *Common Entrance Exam* to go to high school." Martha had stayed home for the first couple of months of the new school year because she did not have the proper uniform. Then Grandma Sutton acquired whatever material she could afford and sewed her uniform. She was only able to make a skirt, and it was a slightly different shade of green from the uniform the other students wore. Martha was still happy that she was finally able to start school; but that happiness was short-lived. The teacher made a spectacle of Martha in front of the class on her first day, leaving her feeling humiliated and dejected. She felt like she did not belong there; but she did her best to catch up on her own, knowing she had to pass the exam within another couple of months. This would give her the chance to go to high school with Eve, and in the long run, escape the poverty.

At least Eve doesn't have to worry about this sort of thing anymore, Martha thought. Martha missed Eve. Eve was living with Grandma Sutton, but Martha had to stay with Grandma Martin during the week to go to the nearby school. It had only been a few months since their mom had relocated to America – to make a better life for them they were told. The plan was for her to come back and get them as soon as she could. Martha missed her mom, but part of her was relieved that she would no longer have to worry about the instability. She and Eve were born in the Bahamas and first went to Jamaica when they were only a few months old. They lived with their mom and maternal grandmother, Grandma Martin, for about a year. Shortly after that, their mom took them back to live in The Bahamas for another year. At age three, Martha's mom relocated to Jamaica for good, where they again lived with Grandma Martin. Then when Martha was around age four, she and Eve were sent to live with their dad and stepmother for a short while due to some financial difficulties their mom was having. This was a sad time for Martha. She and Eve were not allowed to call their father 'Dad.' Their stepmother insisted they called him 'Uncle Alan' since that was what her children from a previous relationship called him. Martha greatly resented that, but she quietly did what she was told. Martha wondered why her dad never stood up for her and Eve and insisted that they use his proper title.Her stepmother also happened to be her teacher at the school they attended. One afternoon Martha fell asleep in class. Her stepmother woke her up and told her to go and run around the school. She was still groggy from having just awakened, and did not feel like running. Moreover, she was more than a little embarrassed. She started jogging a bit, but not running full out. That incurred her stepmother's wrath, and Martha got a whipping in school that day. Then she had to go home and be chastised by her father about the same incident. To Martha, there seemed no escape from the constant sadness.

On the night their mom returned to take them back home to live with her, Martha overheard a huge quarrel outside the gate. She and Eve were told to get dressed so they could go home. They put on their matching yellow and white dresses and had their little bags packed. But as they were about to step through the door, the argument escalated between the adults and their stepmother slammed the door shut and told them to go to bed.

They finally went back home after months, but Martha experienced a different kind of distress there. Her mom used to spend a lot of time with her best friend, Aunt Tina. She would get dressed in the evenings and leave, and she would not come back until late at nights. Martha and Eve would stand on their bed and peek out the window for what seemed like hours. To pass the time while they waited, they would sing. *A little More Oil in my Lamp* was one of their favorites. They had learned it at church. Then every night starting at 6 o'clock, they would sit by the kerosine lamp for hours and read the Psalms out loud for Grandma Martin. Owing to that, Martha learned to recite most of the Psalms word for word, which brought her great comfort.

Montvale was not very different from Baker's Town where Grandma Sutton lived. The streets were cleaner in Montvale, but the constant in both communities was the violence during the time of political elections. The sound of gunshots could be heard at nights, creating a certain amount of dread in Martha. At a young age she had witnessed a thug on the street carrying a barely concealed machine gun with the muzzle sticking out of a brown paper bag. She had seen people shot and killed right in her neighborhood. Martha's stomach growled and she was reminded that she did not have anything to eat that morning. Grandma Martin was getting older and could not sell at the market anymore, and there was no one in the household who held a regular job.

"Martha, come here to me." The sound of Grandma Martin's voice jolted Martha out of her reverie. "Did you call me, Grandma?" Martha hurried over to where her grandmother was sitting on the edge of the bed looking out the front door.

"Go over to Mr. Linn's shop and give him this list. Tell him I am asking him to trust me these items, and I will pay him when my daughter sends me some money from America."

Martha ran over to Mr. Linn's shop, hoping that school would not let out before she was finished with the task. She was afraid the children would come into the shop and she would have to wait until everyone left before she gave Grandma Martin's message to the shop-keeper. She had done it often, and it was more embarrassing every time. Grayson was proud as a young boy, and he simply refused to go to the shop to credit groceries anymore. Today, the shop was crowded and Martha tarried at the back like she always did. "Can I help the next person?" called Mr. Linn. Martha hesitantly edged her way toward the counter and whispered, "My grandma told me to give you this note; she said she will pay you when she gets some money."

Mr. Linn looked annoyed, and Martha knew that was probably because her grandmother already owed Mr. Linn some money from the week before. Without saying a word, Mr. Linn turned around and started packing the groceries into a brown paper bag. He wrapped one pound of flour, one pound of sugar, half a loaf of bread, and an ounce of butter. Then he added a can of sardines, and a quarter bottle of cooking oil. Grateful that school was still in session, Martha thanked Mr. Linn for the groceries and hefted the brown paper bag up against her chest. *At least there will be something to eat for dinner,* she thought to herself as she jogged back to the house with the grocery bag held securely in her arms. *I don't have to worry about Eve; she has food tonight,* thought Martha. Martha hummed to herself, feeling happy that they would have dinner that night.

Within days however, their meager supplies were used up and Grandma Martin turned to the neighbors for help this time. *Here we go again,* Martha said to herself as she meandered down the road to borrow money from Ms. Hyacinth. When she returned a short time later, she had to deliver the bad news to Grandma Martin. "Grandma, Ms. Hyacinth says she does not have any money." Grandma Martin just nodded and started singing out loud. "Jehovah Jireh, my provider..." As she belted out the notes in her strong alto voice, Martha said a prayer that God would send someone who could lend Grandma Martin some money so they would not have to go to bed hungry that night.

For Martha, hunger was not the worst thing about living in Montvale; it was the sense of insecurity she felt. They lived in a one-room house with about 20 square feet of living space. There were 14 people living in the house, so they were taught to be careful of even those who lived inside the home. Grandma Martin lived there with Aunt Meg and her three children, one of whom was sick his entire life. Aunt Meg's son rarely ever spoke, never learned to bathe and feed himself, and never went to school. Aunt Nola's three boys also lived in the home as their mother was living in America. These boys were teenagers when Martha was a little girl. Then there was Uncle Clyde who was Grandma Martin's youngest son. Martha's mom and her four children also lived in this single room: that included Martha, her two sisters and one older brother. There were four beds – one in each corner of the room. Martha and her two sisters slept on a full-sized bed with Grandma Sutton; they used to share this bed with their mom before she left for the States. Her brother Grayson, slept on a twin bed in the diagonal corner of the room with Uncle Clyde. Aunt Meg and her children slept on the third bed; and Aunt Nola's three boys slept on the fourth bed. The sleeping arrangement was not ideal, but they made space for everyone the best they could. Then Uncle John's house burned down and he came knocking on the door in the middle of the night looking for a place to stay. Uncle John had come to live with them too; he slept in an enclosed area near the bathroom in the back of the house. Sometimes he slept outside, and Martha feared that someone might hold him at gunpoint one night and make him ask to be let inside. This was what the adults feared based on their whispered conversations.

The threat of danger was always there, from inside the home and from outside. At nights, Martha would have nightmares about someone breaking into the home through the wooden doors whose locks were barely able to keep the door closed. Grandma Martin would fuss with Uncle Clyde constantly because he stayed out late on the streets and came home at 3:00 in the morning on a regular basis. She was afraid that at some point burglars would follow him home. This was the whisperings of the adults at any rate. They secretly called him *three o'clock Clyde*. He never worked as far as Martha knew; a neighbor had hit him in the spine with a rock when he was a young boy and he was handicapped for the rest of his life. One foot was turned at an unusual angle so that he walked on his ankle with a very distinct limp. He was a very angry person; he would rant and rave at Grandma Martin frequently, throwing out curse words indiscriminately. He also got into frequent altercations with neighbors as well as other family members.

One night, Martha's greatest fear became a reality. Around 3:30 in the morning right after Uncle Clyde came in, someone started breaking down the back door of their house. All the adults started screaming, "Help! Murder! Rape!" Their grandmother shoved Martha and her two sisters under the bed and scooted in with them, using her body as a shield. Martha said a prayer as they huddled there in the dark for what seemed like hours. The burglar ended up running away when their cousin threatened to shoot. Since then, Martha would have recurring

SHATTERED BUT SHELTERED

nightmares of huge boulders coming at her and going down her throat, threatening to choke her.

It was only a few weeks later that Martha witnessed a man gunned down in the street around the corner from their home. When they heard the shots, all the adults started running toward the sound, shouting, "They killed Mr. Tom's son!" It was close to the 1980 election, and the violence was rampant. Martha was terrified! She did not want to go to the scene, but she was afraid to stay at the house alone, so she followed the crowd. When she got there, a man was languishing in the street, his white shirt covered in blood, and his body in a contorted position. There were American soldiers camped out in the school nearby who were there to keep the peace, but this did not stop the violence. People were killed just for sporting the wrong color clothing in certain communities. That night the dream came again, and Martha awakened with a start, sweat soaking her brow. As she awakened, she found herself in a puddle. To her dismay, she realized she had wet the bed yet again. She felt like she was the only big girl who was still wetting the bed.

It was not long after that incident that Martha was awakened in the middle of the night to a loud, blaring noise. There was a bright light shining into the house through the windows and the trees outside were swaying wildly. When she peeked outside, a helicopter was hovering directly above the mango tree in the front yard with the search lights sweeping back and forth the around the yard. It turned out it was a military helicopter; apparently there was someone on the run and they suspected the person had run into the yard. Martha was so frightened; she thought it was the end of the world.

Martha was relieved when Fridays came and she would get on the bus to go and spend the weekend at Grandma Suttons' house. This weekend she was anxious to see Eve. Baker's Town was the better of the two evils. At least she would not be hungry. There was always food at Grandma Sutton's house; Martha's dad sent money to Grandma Sutton often, and when he could not, his brothers and sisters did. As she pushed the large iron gates open, the barking dogs gave her a sense of security. "Hey sis!" exclaimed Eve, as she sprinted around the corner from the back of the yard. They threw their arms around each other in an emotional embrace. They shared stories about their week and giggled with glee. But the weekend ended all to quickly and Martha had to make her way back to Montvale.

That year, Martha passed the *Common Entrance Exam.* She had begged her classmates for help whenever possible, and worked hard to get to high school despite the challenges. She skipped fifth and sixth grade and went straight to seventh grade. She was rewarded by going to live with Grandma Sutton full-time along with Eve. Martha felt bad leaving Connie and Grayson behind. Grayson had it very hard; he was forced to go to school barefooted when he had outgrown his only pair of shoes. Due to lack of funds, he also had to wear short pants to school instead of the long khaki pants that were required as part of the uniform. After a while he just refused to go to school because he could not stand the embarrassment. He and Connie had to remain with Grandma Martin. Whenever Martha sat down to have a meal, she would say a prayer that Grayson and Connie had food to eat as well.

To Martha, life in Baker's Town was not so bad once she was inside the gates of their residence. Their father was now in The States, but he would call every now and then and say hello to them. Martha did not know her dad very well. Her only memory of him was when she and Eve lived with him for that short time.

SHATTERED BUT SHELTERED

Grandma Sutton's house held some good memories in spite of its undesirable location. Grandma Sutton was stern, but she was never unkind. Grandpa Sutton was quiet; he said very little, but Martha knew he loved having her and Eve around. Aunt Diane was Grandpa Sutton's sister, and she was blind from the time Martha first met her. Prior to losing her sight, she was an avid reader. Aunt Diane would sit down with Martha and Eve in the evenings and recite stories and poems word-for-word from memory. She was a very smart lady, who was also very proper. If Martha or Eve used the local dialect, Aunt Diane would ask in the sweetest voice, "Which dictionary did you find that word in?" This would make them giggle, but they would be sure to use proper English whenever they were around her.

Grandma Sutton sent Martha and her sister to church every weekend. The church was next door to their house, and they walked over on Saturday mornings. They made many friends and enjoyed taking part in the services. They learned to sing in front of the congregation very early on. They went to prayer meetings on Wednesday nights as well. One Wednesday night, Martha sat near the rear doors inside the church enjoying the service. Eve was right beside her as always. A young man discreetly slipped into the seat on the other side of Eve and gently placed the M-16 he was carrying on the ground between his legs. Martha froze! But the elder continued his exhortation, and the other church members continued their praise as if there was nothing amiss. After a few minutes, the young man got up, picked up his weapon and left as quietly as he had come. Eve later learned from the whisperings of the adults that he was being chased by bad guys and he came into the church to dodge them, then left when they had passed by.

Baker's Town was a rough neighborhood. Taxi drivers refused to go in there. They would drop their passengers off at the police station near the entrance to the town, and they would walk the rest of the way to their destination. Martha and Eve once went with their aunt to visit someone in a nearby hospital. A man who was seated next to them in the waiting room asked where they were from. When they told him they were from Baker's Town, the man replied with genuine wonder in his voice, "I didn't know anything good could come out of Baker's Town." The reality is, many good people came out of Baker's Town.

On Friday nights, the church members would join the Suttons in their home for worship to open the Sabbath. They would sit on the long wooden benches that Grandpa Sutton made and sing songs that would ring out around the neighborhood. Then they would read the scriptures and pray. This was a regular occurrence, and Martha learned to enjoy the routine. She looked forward to the Sabbath, which was filled with joy. There was a sense of peacefulness on that day, when no one did homework or went to the store. They would go to church in the morning, then have a nice lunch at home or at the home of a friend while they listened to inspirational music playing in the background. Then they would go back to church for the youth program in the afternoon.

One evening they were eating dinner when the gunshots started to ring out just outside the house. Everyone got down on the ground and waited with baited breaths for things to settle down. Footsteps could be heard running, and to Martha's dismay, the gate opened and the footsteps came closer. It became quiet outside, but heavy, labored breathing could be heard as someone entered the yard and ran toward the back of the house. The dogs barked incessantly, and Martha peeked out the window. As things quieted down, her uncles and aunts went out to see what was going on. Apparently, a guy from the

SHATTERED BUT SHELTERED

streets was shot in the leg and ran into the yard to take shelter. When they found him, he was perched on top of the zinc fence waiting to see if his assailant was gone. With blood pouring from his wound, he was quickly loaded into a car by a family friend and taken to the local hospital.

Martha got used to the surroundings, and was soon settled into the upscale Catholic high school. Quite a few American children attended school there, and they lived in the boarding school that was on the premises. To Martha, it seemed most of the children at her school did well financially; but things were sometimes difficult for Grandma Sutton. Most of the time Martha would get .35 cents for lunch. That could buy her a sugar bun and a bottle of juice. When Grandma Sutton did not have enough money, she would pack plantain sandwiches for Martha and Eve to take to school for lunch, and their beverage was water. Martha was sometimes embarrassed to pull out her bread and plantain when the other children were eating their hot lunches. Instead of sitting in the lunch room, she would walk around the school yard at lunch time, and eat out of the brown paper bag while she walked. She walked alone because she did not have many friends. Eve was in a different class and took lunch at a separate time.

There was one girl in Martha's class who used to bully her. She called her names, and made fun of her every day. One day as Martha was walking around the school yard eating her lunch, this girl gathered her friends and started following Martha around. They laughed and teased that she had peed on herself. Martha ignored them; but afterward, she went to the bathroom to check on what they were laughing at. That is when she noticed that the soap she had used on her legs that morning in place of lotion, had washed down her legs when she perspired. This did not stop Martha from getting her education, however. She was told often that that education was the way to get out of poverty.

Despite the struggles, the stability counted for something. Martha and Eve thrived considerably in the four years they spent in Baker's Town. They formed great relationships with their aunts and uncles – their dad's siblings who were living at Grandma Sutton's at the time. These were the five youngest siblings out of ten, their father and his twin being the eldest. In fact, Martha developed much closer bonds with her aunts and uncles than she did with her father. During the years in Baker's Town, she received unmatched love and care from her family. They would make sure Martha and Eve had decent clothes to wear and enough food to eat. Martha grew to love the people in the community as well, and the church became an integral part of their lives. Yet the joy they felt when their mom finally returned to take them to America with her was immeasurable.

———

Martha used to think America was up in the air because that is where the airplanes went. She could barely contain her excitement as she sat on the gigantic aircraft next to Eve. "I can't wait to take off," exclaimed Grayson, bouncing up and down in his seat across the aisle from Martha. "I can't wait to see what our new house looks like," returned Martha. Eve sighed, and a dreamy look came into her eyes. "I can't wait for us girls to have our own room, and I want to try all the different foods," she said. Connie had to stay behind in Jamaica because their mom did not have enough money to purchase all four airline tickets. This was another blow for Connie who felt that she always got the short end of the stick. But she was the most logical person to leave behind since Martha and Eve were Bahamians and were traveling on their mom's passport. Grayson was the eldest, but he had just gotten into a scuffle with the neighborhood boys and had been stabbed in the stomach with a knife. Their mom was afraid he would not survive long enough to relocate to America. Martha was glad to be reunited with her siblings, and she was excited that they would finally be together as a family despite this little glitch. Connie would be able to join them within a week, and Martha could not wait.

———————∿∿∿———————

Moving to a new country was very exciting, but it also took some adjustment. The first thing Martha learned was just how vast America was; she was fascinated by the bright lights and big cities. The culture was very different from what Martha was used to. As Martha approached her ninth-grade classroom on the first day of class, she was filled with nervous excitement. She liked school, but she was nervous about fitting in and making friends. Martha knocked on the big, heavy door, and a tall blond guy opened the classroom door. "Good morning," said Martha. The boy did not answer, and Martha soon discovered that he was a student. It took her by surprise to see that the ninth- grade students were a few years older than she was on average. The teacher was sitting at a desk on the far side of the room. Martha walked over and repeated the greeting which was meant for the teacher in the first place. Everything about America was different: From the food, to the people, to the way students addressed teachers. Young children smoked in the corridors at school, and some were seen making out in the hallways. Martha was not used to seeing that; where she came from, children did not smoke, and most high-school aged children did not hook up. She found the coursework much easier than what she was working on in Jamaica. She was far ahead of the curve in most subjects, but struggled in American History. Yet she still managed to make a B average in her weakest subject.

The financial struggles continued at home, but Martha remained focused on her academics with the single-minded goal of escaping poverty. Grocery shopping was always a big production. They were on food stamps and Martha was glad they would not have to go hungry anymore. But it was a bit embarrassing to go to the grocery store. They would buy groceries in bulk because they did not have transportation to make multiple trips. One night they were pushing their grocery cart home because the bus had stopped running for the night, and they did not have enough money to take a taxi. They had about a 20-minute walk down a busy street, and there was no pavement. They took turns pushing the cart on the grass shoulder on the side of the road, and when it became unbearable, they would edge closer to the white line to push it on the pavement for a while when traffic slowed down. As they got closer to the road, a man passing by in his car spit on them through window, yelling a racial slur at them as he went by. It was a very helpless feeling.

Martha did not know that she was Black until she came to the United States. In Jamaica she attended high school with White children, but there was no distinction between them. Skin color was something people did not think twice about in her culture. As she assimilated into the American culture she came to learn that people were classified more by race than by class as was the case in Jamaica. It was a bit disconcerting, but Martha remained true to who she was, and treated people like people. She learned to love individuals for who they were, and not for what they looked like.

Within months of arriving in the United States, instability reared its ugly head in Martha's life again. The threat of being evicted from their home became very real, as Martha's mom resigned from her live-in job shortly after they came to live with her. Her mom used to care for an old lady in one of the high-rise buildings on the beach. She would stay there for work all week and come home on the weekends, so Martha and her sisters would care for themselves during the week. Grayson did not go to school; the plan was for him to learn a trade. Grayson would make sure that Martha and her sisters got out on time for school in the mornings. Martha's mom soon quit her job, explaining that someone she knew threatened to call the authorities and inform them that she was leaving the children unsupervised at nights. This sent the family into another tailspin, as Martha's mom did not have enough money to pay the rent. The landlady threatened to put their things out on the sidewalk after repeated attempts to collect the rent, which by then had not been paid for months. Martha and her sisters became the messengers; they sometimes had to make excuses to the landlady about why their mom was not available to talk to her.

Six months after arriving in the U.S. the family split up again. This would set into motion a series of events that sent Martha and each of her siblings on a different path. Martha and Connie were sent off to the north to live with their dad and stepmother again. Grayson and Connie were sent to the north as well to live with their mom's sister, Aunt Penny. Grayson refused to go back to high school; he had missed so much time in school and felt like he was too old to be in high school and that the children would make fun of him. He chose instead to go out on the streets and try to make some fast money. Connie continued living with Aunt Penny who was a kind woman. But the home was over-crowded with little adult supervision. A few months after moving north, Connie was sent back to Jamaica in shame and humiliation to live with Grandma Martin again. It was about a year before their mom sorted out the finances somewhat and could bring Connie back to the U.S.

Martha and Eve had an advantage, because they had their father's side of the family which offered a bit more stability. Going back to live with their dad was not the best situation, but at least they were together and could support each other. Martha spent her 10th grade year in a high school in the north, then she and all her siblings were reunited once again with their mom in the south. Martha spent her 11th grade year back in the south. Coming back together was great, but this time Martha was not very confident that things would remain that way. It did not take her by surprise when they were evicted from their new apartment. Then their mom rented a 3-bedroom house from one of their church brothers. She was still having difficulty keeping a job, and this arrangement was short-lived. By that time, Martha was in 12th grade and Eve had been granted a full scholarship to a local college. They continued to attend church regularly and made some very good friends along the way. Sometimes they caught the bus to church, and sometimes they were picked up by other church members. The man they rented from spread the news throughout the church that Martha's mom was not paying the rent. Martha was subjected to shame and humiliation among her friends, and eventually they were evicted.

Right after that, Martha's mom rented a room in the home of a friend. Martha received a full scholarship to the same college Eve attended and now they were both living on campus. They spent the weekends at home, however. The landlady sublet the rooms in the house to other renters. Martha and her family had the use of one bedroom along with a small den area. They had their own bathroom, but they had to share a kitchen with the landlady and two other renters. One afternoon, Martha was lying on the bed with a leg propped on the window which opened toward the side of the house. Suddenly, she felt a sharp tug on her leg, as a man from outside started dragging her out the open window. She started screaming, and her mother came running to her rescue. The man let go and took off. That was a very peculiar incident. Martha's mom reported it to the police, but they never found the perpetrator.

They were watching the news together one night and a familiar face came up on the screen. Martha recognized Kent, one of the young men who was renting a room in the same house they occupied. Kent would often wait for Martha and Eve to head out to the bus stop, then he would leave right behind them and offer them a ride in his car. Of course, they would always refuse, but he would just try again the next week when they were heading back to campus. The newscaster reported that Kent was in custody and was being charged with armed robbery of a local fast-food restaurant. The police had caught him in another state heading north. They reported that he had a prior criminal record and was wanted in another state for sexual assault of a child. They were shaken by the fact that they lived in the same house with a criminal. But they remained focused on their quest for an education, all the time being aware that this was their only way out of this dreaded cycle of hardship.

That incident coupled with the fact that they could not pay the rent led to them move from this location into a house next door to the church they attended. They called it the church house because the property was owned by the church. To help her pay the rent, the church hired Martha's mom as the custodian. Martha and her siblings were all part of the work team; they essentially cleaned the church in exchange for a place to stay. They would start cleaning the church on Saturday nights after all the members had left, and finish up on Sundays. Then they would clean up again after the Wednesday night service, and get the property ready for Sabbath services. Martha's mom had some interpersonal conflicts with some of the church members, and they would regularly smear filth all over the bathrooms and leave if for them to clean. This became humiliating for Martha and her siblings. Grayson, who had returned from the north to live with the family decided this was too much and left again to go back north. It was right after that that he got in trouble with the law, and was convicted on a drug charge involving a weapon. After serving his time, he was deported to Jamaica, leaving five young children from three different mothers.

Martha and her sisters did not have a choice. They were too young to leave home, so they stuck it out through the difficult times. Even with the income from the custodian job, Martha's mom was still unable to cover the rent. To supplement that, Eve who was now 17, took a job as the pastor's secretary while she attended college full-time. Eve's entire paycheck went toward the rent. Martha also found a job while attending college. She would work 20 hours a week, and catch three buses to travel from her job back to the campus every day. Martha's paychecks went into buying groceries for the family and helping with the utilities. Every Friday evening when she got paid, she would come home on the bus with bags of groceries. Then she would walk the five blocks from the bus stop, both arms loaded with grocery bags. Martha felt a great deal of strain from the responsibility of providing for the entire family. She was still in her first year of college, so she did not have much hope for escape. She continued buying groceries and paying bills in the home without complaining; but secretly, she longed for the opportunity to leave home as quickly as possible.

Chapter 2
SHELTER IN THE STORM

THE DINGY MOTEL room had now become strangely familiar. Martha felt bored with the monotony of the sexual interlude, but that was not unusual. While she was physically present, her mind was otherwise engaged. How in the world did I get myself into this situation again, she wondered grimly, as she reflected on the cycle she had been stuck in for the past 16 years. She was searching for something that was constantly out of her reach. She futilely sought confirmation that she was 'normal,' and that she could learn to enjoy the sexual act despite what had happened.

This dreadful cycle began in a motel room much like the one where Martha now found herself. It was a few months into the Fall semester, and Martha was still getting used to campus life. Home was not far away; but Martha did not have transportation, and staying on campus meant not having to travel to school by bus every day. She did not mind the experience of living on campus where everything was new and exciting. Having been raised in a Christian home, she was sheltered and did not have the social skills typical of other teens her age. Her upbringing was very conservative such that she did not wear make-up nor jewelry; but more importantly, she was raised with certain core values around spirituality, justice, compassion, fairness and self-respect. In her early years, she also developed strong values surrounding family, achievement, honesty, patience, perseverance and faith.

Life was not always easy, as Martha was forced to deal with deprivation at a very young age. While she had learned early to be content with little, she could not come to terms with the violence she had witnessed on a regular basis. Even though she had lived in impoverished, crime-ridden neighborhoods, she was not allowed to mingle with the other children there. She had kept herself circumspect, and was not touched by the delinquency that was so prevalent in her immediate surroundings. She was not exposed to television for the first ten years of her life, as her family could not afford one. When she had gone to live with her paternal grandmother around age 10, crime was rampant there as well, but she was grateful that they had a bit more financial means than she was used to. She could watch wholesome programs on their black and white television which was turned on only on weekends. This did not do Martha any harm, as she became creative in making her own toys, and developed a love for books. She was trained to focus on her studies, and came to see education as her only way to escape the poverty that was all around her. As such, she excelled in school and became active in the church. She had become baptized at age 10 and was always excited about participating in church programs. This formed the foundation of her faith, and continued to influence her life even after she was reunited with her mother and her other siblings.

At age 16, Martha was innocent in every sense of the word. However, it was not lost on her at the time that she was one of the more attractive girls on campus. Having skipped two years of high school, she was younger than the average college freshman and smart as a whip. She received a great deal of attention from the opposite sex. Her suitors were not only college students, but they included men from the neighborhood who came by to scope out the 'new blood' as the incoming students were commonly called. Being so sheltered, she did not have much experience with boys. While she was flattered by the attention she received, she was also quite overwhelmed. There were times when she found herself in a quandary as to how to handle all the attention.

That fateful Friday night was outside of the norm in many ways. Since the college campus was only about 30 miles from home, Martha usually went home every weekend with her sister, Eve. The main reason for going home was so that they could properly observe the Sabbath with their family as they were accustomed to doing. That weekend Martha and her sister stayed on campus. The reason was two-fold: They were more than a little curious as to what campus life was like on the weekends; and they were not able to go home that weekend even if they wanted to. Their mother was a single parent who often struggled to make ends meet. That weekend, they were being evicted from their home, and everything at home was turned upside down. For the latter reason, their younger sister, Connie was sent to the campus to stay with them even though it was against the school rules.

Things seemed to be progressing as expected until about 8:30 p.m. when Martha decided to go out and get Connie something to eat. As she headed out toward the campus café, commonly referred to as *The Sub*, her conscience screamed at her that it was not necessary to purchase food on the Sabbath, a day on which they avoided all secular activities. She justified her actions by the fact that her sister was hungry. Surely, there could be no harm in getting her something to eat on the Sabbath, Martha reasoned. As she approached *The Sub*, she felt an arm come around her shoulder from behind, and the person began walking alongside her toward *The Sub*. She quickly recognized the person as Owen, a guy who frequented the campus, but was not a student there. She had engaged in brief conversations with him several times on campus, but she did not know much about him. What she knew was that he was very handsome, had light brown eyes, and was quite a smooth talker. She also knew he was 23 years old and lived nearby; but that was the extent of her familiarity with Owen.

As Owen walked with her toward the Sub, his arm tightened around her shoulders. The stench of alcohol was strong on his breath, as he began to tell her in a strangely slurring voice that he had come to the dorm earlier looking for her. She did not recall telling him which dorm she lived in, so she asked him how he knew where to find her. "You told me," he replied. This baffled Martha a bit, but then things became even more peculiar. When they reached the entrance to *The Sub*, Owen continued pulling her along. His arm was now tightening threateningly around her neck, and she realized that she was in real danger.

Martha felt the beginnings of panic, but tried to stay calm and to have a reasonable conversation with Owen. "Where were you going?" asked Owen. "I was headed to *The Sub* to get my sister something to eat," she replied. Owen continued a steady stream of conversation as if to keep Martha distracted, but what he was saying was not getting through to her. She was in full panic mode when she realized she was alone in the back of the building, being steadily propelled along despite her protests. Owen was trying to cajole her into going somewhere with him, but he was not being clear as to where.

She knew she was in trouble when she saw a car parked outside the fence at the rear of the campus. "I cannot go with you!" she screamed, but by now she was not within earshot of anyone on campus. Owen shoved her unceremoniously into the car through the driver's door, and slid in behind her around the steering wheel. The car appeared to be an older model dark brown Buick, where the front seat was all-in-one with no middle console. He shoved her over toward the middle of the seat, but kept his arm tightly wrapped around her neck. He flipped the locks shut and started the engine, all the while keeping one arm slung around her shoulder and his forearm across her neck. All the while, Martha was screaming, "Where are you taking me?" "I need to get back to campus." "My sisters will be looking for me." These were the days before cell phones, and Martha had no way to communicate to her sisters that she was in danger.

Martha was not sure how much time had passed before Owen pulled the car into the parking lot of an apartment building. She was busy tightening the belt on her knee-length white shorts in a futile attempt to protect herself from whom she now recognized as a predator. "Where are we, and what are you doing?" she asked. "I am supposed to pick up a friend here," he replied. It so happened the friend was not there, so he left after tooting the horn a few times. Martha was not sure where she was, but she sought an opportunity for escape anyway. The car doors were locked however, and Owen still had his arm around her neck.

Soon he pulled up at the front of a dingy motel, which seemed to be in the middle of nowhere. Bile arose in Martha's throat and her mouth went dry. She had so many plans for her life, and she felt like all her dreams were about to slip away. Most of all, however, she feared for her life. She felt that if she tried to escape and failed, she would anger her assailant and cause him to inflict bodily harm. She tried reasoning with him again and again to take her back to campus, but with no success.

It appeared he had rented the room ahead of time, because he took her directly to a room on the second floor without stopping in the office of the motel. Carefully sliding the dead bolt in place, he locked the door behind them with a key and removed the key from the lock. From that moment on, Martha found herself engaged in a strenuous physical battle as Owen fought to strip her of her clothes. The struggle continued for what seemed like hours, but there is no telling how much time had passed. She screamed at the top of her lungs until her throat hurt, but no one came to her rescue. If anyone heard they did not seem to care. Eventually Owen's strength prevailed. Being a virgin at the time, she could not physically accommodate him. He became very angry, accusing her of purposely making it difficult. He attempted to lubricate her in ways that were utterly shocking to Martha, and forced her to reciprocate. He

SHATTERED BUT SHELTERED

assaulted her repeatedly, keeping his hand around her throat the entire time in a menacingly threatening gesture.

Martha looked around for something she could use to deliver a fatal blow. All she had at her disposal was the lamp on the desolate beside table and a hairpin that had been dislodged from her hair. She was terrified of even trying to injure him, because she instinctively knew that if she tried and failed he would surely kill her. Thus, she remained immobile, doing nothing. He kept her restrained when he dozed, but she stayed awake all night thinking of a way to escape. He would awake numerous times just to assault her again. She felt weak from the exertion of trying to fight off her assailant, so she finally just gave up fighting and resigned herself to her fate. The physical pain was almost unbearable. She was disgusted by the scent of his body, and eventually she became like a zombie, unable to feel anything anymore. She could not even begin to wrap her mind around what was happening; all she could do was hope she would come out of it alive. She stayed awake until finally she saw the first signs of dawn. Owen raped her again then he put her into the shower and made her wash herself off. It was only as Martha was recounting the story so many years later that she realized the significance of him putting her into the shower that morning; that would remove all evidence of their sexual encounter.

At about 8 *o'clock* the next morning Owen brought Martha back to the campus as if nothing had happened. The icing on the cake was when he dropped her off at the back gate of the school. "Do you have money?" he asked. "I have $5 for groceries" she replied, and he laughed. To Martha, that seemed like a very strange way to part after the life-changing events of the night before. She remembers thinking to herself that this seemed like a very normal occurrence to him.

Martha ran into a police officer outside the dorm as she made her way to her room. The officer asked her name, indicating that her sisters had reported her missing. She spoke with the officer alone and told him she was fine. She was still in a state of shock, and she did not quite know what to say. What she did not tell the police was that she was kidnapped for 12 hours and sexually assaulted. What she remembers most about the encounter with the police officer is that he responded as if to a vagrant who had run off for a night of fun and entertainment. That broke Martha's heart. He did not even ask how old she was or what had happened. All the officer said to her was, "Next time, tell someone where you are going." There was no report or paperwork filed. It was much later in life that she learned that at the age of 16, even if she had consented, the incident should have been treated as statuary rape at the very least.

Martha's sisters and her aunt were waiting for her upstairs when she made her way inside the dorm. Martha was in a bit of a fog when she was reunited with her family. She remembered her aunt asking, "Why do you look so dirty?" She was disheveled: Her hair was undone, her belt was missing, her blouse was hanging outside of her shorts, and her white shorts were filthy from rolling around on the floor of the motel room. One of her roommates whispered to the other, "It looks like someone had a run-in last night." Martha did not know what to make of that; she just assumed that these things happened on college campuses and she just had to go on. It was not that simple, however. From that point on, her whole world had changed drastically – just how much, she would only come to realize in the weeks and months ahead.

The weeks that followed were excruciatingly painful ones. Martha begged her mother not to file a report with the police because of the shame and guilt she felt. She was afraid all her church friends and family would find out, and she would have been subjected to more embarrassment. Yet, she secretly hoped her mother would have reported it despite her protests. She felt like she had become an adult overnight, and that her life had changed dramatically. She felt like a different person altogether, as if her eyes were suddenly opened and she saw the world in a whole new light. But even then, she had a quiet determination within, that none of the plans she had made prior to the incident would be derailed. She knew the expectations her family had for her, and was resolute that she would not disappoint herself and her family.

Her mother took her to numerous medical appointments, but it was too early to determine whether she was pregnant. The doctor diagnosed that her hymen was broken. This was difficult to reconcile. Inside, she felt like her entire world had just been shattered, and she was feeling utterly devastated. She was given a little pink pill and told it might abort the fetus in case one should form. She was then given a 30-day follow-up appointment. She was also tested for sexually transmitted diseases, including HIV, with another 30-day waiting period for the results. During that time, her anxiety mounted to peak levels. This marked the beginning of a serious battle with anxiety which would only manifest further down the road. However, Martha was not aware of that at the time; she was just trying to survive one day at a time.

To Martha, the events that followed were like being stuck in a whirlwind; or being tossed back and forth in a storm with no way of escape. She watched daily as her normally slender body began to change shape; her stomach started to round out and her waist started to thicken. Her breasts became tender and just a tad bit rounder. It may not have been obvious to an onlooker, but she noticed that her clothes were fitting a bit snug around the waist. She wanted to cry, but she could not afford herself that luxury; she had to focus on school and continue the quest for her degree. She did not want to believe it, but she could not deny the reality of what was happening. She just kept putting one foot in front of the other however, taking one day at a time.

When she finally received the test results it turned out that she was indeed pregnant. This served to shatter the rest of her already broken dreams. She silently mourned the fact that she would no longer be able to have the life she had dreamed of; to be a virgin when she got married; to have a family that would be together forever. She had dreams of having twins, since her father was a twin; but that might not come to pass. Then she was forced to do what was taboo in the eyes of her family and friends, as well as the church. Her mother decided that she should have an abortion so as not to interrupt her education and derail a very promising career. Martha did not even think to argue.

On that fateful Friday morning, Martha and her mother got dressed and took the bus to the clinic. They traveled in silence, but there was a sense of foreboding in the air. Her mother never said much about the incident; she never blamed Martha, but she never asked how she was feeling either. They went in through the back door of a single-story building, and

SHATTERED BUT SHELTERED

Martha felt like a lamb being led to the slaughter. She knew what had to be done, but she was nervous about the procedure, not knowing what to expect.

The abortion was not only physically excruciating, but emotionally distressing as well. This came exactly two months after President Reagan had announced to pro-life activists in July 1987 that the federal government would no longer fund counseling and referrals for abortion services under the Title 10 program. Many clinics continued performing the procedures with minimal resources. No general anesthesia was administered. Martha was given a medication that made her feel slightly woozy; yet she was conscious of everything that was taking place and powerless to say she was in excruciating pain. It felt as if someone used a metal object and impaled her, then turned on a vacuum on the end of it. It went on for an indefinite period; she soon lost track of what was taking place as her body went into shock. Eventually she went limp; she felt extremely cold, and shivered uncontrollably for what seemed like hours. Finally, she gave in to the fact that there was nothing she could do but endure the agony. She slept after the procedure. After being allowed to recuperate for about four hours, she was released from the clinic. Her mom called a taxi to take them home.

Martha returned to campus on Monday and resumed her studies like nothing had happened; but the guilt and shame that followed was like nothing she had ever experienced. She kept thinking about what she could have done to make the whole scenario turn out differently. Maybe if she had not been such a coward she would have tried to defend herself. She thought about the possibility that if she tried and failed, the assailant might have turned his anger on her and she would no doubt be dead. Yet she could not escape the guilt.

With all the emotions Martha experienced surrounding the incident, she never cried. The only way she knew how to deal with what had transpired was to suppress all the memories of the event and pretend it did not affect her at all. She buried herself into her school work and made straight A's that semester. The next semester she changed her major from Pre-law to Psychology. This was an effort to gain greater insight into human behavior and understand herself better. School became a welcome distraction, and she channelled all her energies into her studies.

As it turned out, Martha made straight A's for four consecutive years, and graduated college summa cum laude with a Bachelors in Community-Clinical Psychology. During that time, she did not discuss the events of her Freshman year with anyone. It was never spoken of again by anyone in her family. The topic was taboo; safely tucked away in a secluded place. It appeared that she was living a normal life after all, until she was sitting at a bus stop outside the school one day, and she saw Owen drive by in his car. She went into full panic mode; her mouth went dry and her heart started pounding. She looked around for a place to run to, but thankfully, he did not stop or attempt to approach her. After that, she never saw Owen again, so she felt safe enough; but the events of the past would all catch up with her soon enough.

Chapter 3
NINE YEARS OF SILENCE

MARTHA WAS VERY pleased with the turn her life had taken. She was now 22 years old, and it had been one year since she had married Mike whom she had met as teenager. She and Mike had dated for three years before they decided to get married in what was really a spur of the moment decision. She had received a full scholarship for the doctoral program at a local university, and so she continued her studies while working the night shift at a state psychiatric hospital.

One morning when her shift was almost over she rushed into the bathroom with a sudden urge to vomit. "Are you alright?" asked her friend Mary. "I have been feeling a bit nauseous lately," replied Martha. I guess I haven't been eating regular meals." This went on for about a week. Then Martha decided to take a home pregnancy test. To her surprise, she was pregnant. She and Mike were happy about the prospect of becoming parents; after all, they did plan to have two children. However, she was in her first semester of graduate school. Being young and naïve, Martha did not think to use birth control while she was in school. Still, they were excited about starting their family together.

Martha was so sick during the pregnancy that she would pull over on the shoulder of the highway to vomit several times before making it to work at midnight. On one occasion, she threw up on the front steps of the hospital on her way in to work. She was just unable to keep her food down despite a valiant effort. After a few months, her employer placed her on the day shift temporarily.

The new schedule worked well for Martha. Her workday ended at 4:00 p.m., and she had to be at school by 4:30 p.m. She would scurry across town from work to school every day. Then she would hustle across campus with her huge stomach, carrying a heavy, old-fashioned briefcase in one hand and a spit cup in the other. She carried the spit cup with her all the time during the first seven months of her pregnancy. She was so nauseous she could not so much as swallow her saliva, so she would sit through classes with her spit cup. On one occasion she was subjected to scrutiny when she went into the school's bookstore with her spit cup and the attendant asked her if was chewing tobacco. She became very annoyed and angrily pointed him to her stomach. With much perseverance, she finished the first semester of her doctoral program at the university, then requested a leave of absence to give birth to her son.

When their son came along Martha dedicated herself to caring for her family. She immensely enjoyed parenting, and was overjoyed when their daughter came along almost four years later. However, the marriage itself was not a bed of roses. Her husband, Mike was battling a very serious drug addiction which included marijuana and crack cocaine as the drugs of choice. She was aware that he had some issues prior to the marriage, but she had no clue as to the extent of his addiction. It really mattered very little to Martha, because getting married was a way to escape the poverty that was so prevalent at home. Leaving home meant not having to worry about when the next eviction notice would come. It meant she would escape the strain of having to buy groceries for the entire household at age 16, and paying for utilities out of her wages from the part-time job she held while in college.

Their daughter was only a few months old when Martha came home from work one morning to find ashes in the bathroom sink. "What's this?" Martha asked, although she already knew the answer. As Mike approached her, the stench of cocaine was unmistakable. Then she saw the drug paraphernalia lying carelessly on the bathroom counter. Martha was livid. She immediately went upstairs and pulled all of Mike's clothes out of the closet. "I want you gone within the hour," she yelled, lugging the heavy bundle down the stairs. "I promise I will go and seek help now, Martha." "I realize that this is getting out of control." Mike pleaded with her to put his clothes away, claiming that he has come to realize how much his habit was affecting his family.

Her marriage to Mike turned out to be a roller coaster. They had some good times when Mike was clean, but most of the time Mike's drug habit kept him away from home for extended periods of time. He admitted to her that during the marriage, he had never gone more than a few months without using. When he used drugs, he would stay away from home until the effects wore off or until he could get another fix. There were times during the marriage when Martha felt extremely lonely and neglected. She would lay awake in bed for hours at nights, wondering where her husband was and worrying about his safety. When she went to church she was frequently alone. She was alone at parent - teacher conferences, birthday parties, football games and gymnastics meets. It became somewhat embarrassing after a while, so she started to make light of the situation by calling herself the single married lady. Yet she was always careful to make things look good on the outside, and they went on like that for years.

It had been nine years since that Martha's life-altering encounter as a teenager. She felt her life was going extremely well, all things considered. She was invigorated as she listened to Professor Calen deliver a stimulating lecture in her Master's level Counseling Psychology class. The university had agreed to hold her spot in the doctoral program for one year while she went out on maternity leave. However, by then her priorities had changed dramatically and she chose to give her full attention to her family. When their son became old enough, she had transferred her credits to another school and enrolled in a Master's program in Counseling Psychology with plans to go on and complete her doctorate later. Mike was her biggest

SHATTERED BUT SHELTERED

cheerleader regarding her education. He always encouraged and supported her in such a way that she felt she could accomplish anything.

As she listened to the professor, she began to reflect on her own life. Students were required to role-play counselors and patients, and those playing the role of patients were instructed to talk about a real-life issue they were dealing with. Martha was assigned to role-play the patient while her classmate, Sara roleplayed the counselor. "Something happened to me when I was a teenager, and sometimes I have a hard time even thinking about it," began Martha. "So, you feel like you are still struggling with this," said Sara, accurately reflecting Martha's words back to her. "Do you want to share with me what happened?" Sara queried. This unleashed a flood of emotions Martha did not know still existed. When Martha opened her mouth to speak, the words got stuck in her throat and would not come out. She felt disoriented and confused, not knowing where to begin. She tried to formulate a coherent sentence and tears started flowing. She quickly excused herself from class and made her way to the bathroom. Sara, who was now getting very concerned, followed her out of the classroom. Soon Martha was sobbing uncontrollably. In that moment, the years of pent-up emotions came back like a flood and engulfed her completely. For nine years she had not mentioned or discussed the incident with anyone; and now at age 25, she was so violently shaken by the pain and distress, it threatened to overwhelm her. She was not able to verbalize what had happened so many years earlier.

The next day, Martha visited her Primary Care provider who referred her to a therapist. The insurance she had at the time would cover only six visits. She went through the motions at each visit, but was not able to connect with the therapist. She felt he just did not understand the depth of her pain. Before long, therapy was over and she had accomplished very little. However, she remained focused on keeping her family functional and helping Mike deal with his addition.

With Mike's consent, she sought help for him on numerous occasions; but he would change his mind as soon as the crisis had passed. One morning after Martha got off work, she found herself sitting in the waiting room of a crisis center with Mike. Mike did not show up for work as expected, and his sister contacted Martha. Martha tried his phone, but Mike refused to answer the phone for hours. This was typical of Mike when he was using; he would turn off his phone and disappear for days sometimes. Eventually Mike picked up the phone and Martha told him to get help or she was leaving. She had threatened to leave him numerous times, only to change her mind when Mike promised he would get help for his drug habit. This time Martha succeeded in dragging him out to the crisis center. The counselors interviewed Mike, then they spent hours completing the necessary paperwork to get him into a 30-day in-patient detox program with a 30-day follow up treatment program. As they sat there, various individuals came in to seek help. Next to Martha was a young man who was apparently under the influence of some sort of substance; he was talking to himself and was not making much sense. Another man entered and he was screaming like a baby, and doubling over as if in physical pain. Martha heard the counselors whispering that he was in withdrawal and needed to be attended to right away. Martha felt out of place and wondered how she ever got to that place in life. When it was time to sign the documents for voluntary enrollment into the program, Mike told Martha he that had changed his mind.

Martha continued to stand by Mike, but it was becoming more and more difficult each day. She would lay awake at night, waiting for that call she knew would come – Mike asking her to come and bail him out of jail, sometimes as far as two hours away from home. She would come home from work in the mornings and stay awake all day taking care of their toddler. When Mike finished work in the afternoons he was supposed to come home and relieve her so she could sleep for a few hours before going back in for the midnight shift. Many times, Mike would show up at 11 o'clock at night after leaving work at 3 o'clock in the afternoon. Martha would regularly return to work without sleeping a wink. This took a toll on her health. She struggled with insomnia to the extent that even when she had the opportunity to sleep, she was not able to. On numerous occasions, Martha would wait for Mike to come home and relieve her, but he would simply not show up. On those nights she would either call out from work, or she would take their son to Mike's sister in the middle of the night so she could go to work.

Soon, items started to disappear from the home – little things at first, then furniture and larger appliances started to disappear. Mike was pawning off their belongings for money to sustain his drug habit. Eventually the pool table disappeared from the recreation room in the basement. Then the Electrolux carpet cleaner disappeared. Mike claimed he loaned it to his brother, but it was never seen again. Soon Martha's wedding ring disappeared.

Mike admitted to Martha that his habit was costing them upwards of $20,000 per year. They agreed that Martha would handle the finances since money was Mike's trigger. However, as soon as he started having cravings, he would start a fight to get the money back under his control. One Sabbath Martha went to church and the Treasurer called her into the office. "I have four tithe checks that have been returned unpaid," he informed her. She was floored, because she was the one writing the checks and she knew there was enough money in the account. It turned out that Mike was pulling the money out of the bank behind her back as soon as she made the deposits. She went to the grocery store one day, and two hours later she took a full cart of groceries to the register. She gave the clerk her debit card, and it was declined – there was no money in the account. Mike had depleted their funds to support his habit. It so happened that a church member was right behind her in line. She tried every card in her wallet, but to no avail. Again, she was subjected to that terrible embarrassment. A few months later, she was sent correspondence from the mortgage company that four mortgage payment checks were returned unpaid and they were on the verge of losing their home. Martha was forced to scramble to get the finances back in order. Again, she insisted that Mike seek help, and still he refused.

They were now into their twelfth year of marriage and things continued to deteriorate. Every time Martha thought Mike had hit rock bottom, he would find a new low. One of those lows came one Sabbath afternoon while Martha was entertaining guests from church for Sabbath lunch. She received a call from the local hospital informing her that Mike was in the emergency room. After disappearing for days, he was picked up in a crack house and taken to the emergency room by ambulance. The hospital informed her that he was exhibiting severe psychotic symptoms, and that he admitted to having smoked marijuana laced with formaldehyde. It is still unclear whether the threat was real or imagined; but Mike told Martha and the hospital staff that the other men in the crack house were trying to rob him. To defend himself, he barricaded himself in a bathroom and broke the toilet bowl to use as a weapon. He ended up with multiple self-inflicted lacerations to his legs, thighs, hands and wrists from the broken toilet bowl. He had also severed some tendons in his fingers and required multiple stitches for his injuries. After spending a few days in the hospital, he was released because the doctors determined he was not a danger to himself or others. Still, this was not enough to deter Mike from using drugs; he again he refused long-term treatment after the crisis had passed.

Mike continued to use, but after that fateful day he was never himself again. The paranoia worsened and he started hallucinating regularly. He started seeing things other people did not see, and he thought men in black cars were following him everywhere he went on the highway. He would claim to see tiny microphones in his car, and thought the government was spying on him. Martha kept Mike's drug habit a secret in a vain attempt to keep their lives looking as normal as possible. She took on the primary responsibility for raising the children, all the while trying to protect them from this dysfunctional life they were inherently a part of. She continued attending social and religious events alone, all the while referring to herself as the single married lady.

The straw that broke the camel's back was when Martha was driving down the street one day with her 8-year-old son. Mike had loaned her his truck to drive that day. Her son picked up a small bag and said, "Mommy, what's this?" It was a bag of marijuana which was carelessly left in the vehicle Mike had given to her to drive. Martha's countenance changed drastically in that moment, and she went home and confronted Mike about it. Here was another moment of crisis, and Mike again promised to seek professional help. That was another empty promise. Soon she started to see some strange characters visiting the house, inquiring about Mike's whereabouts. When she confronted Mike regarding the visitors, he confessed that he was involved in some shady business dealings. He refused to tell her any details, stating that he did not wish to implicate her.

This was the beginning of the end of their marriage. But the irony of it is that Martha was not the one who asked for a divorce. She had deep-rooted values around marriage and family; and even though the situation at home was unbearable, she truly believed in marriage as a life-long commitment. She had made a pledge to God that she would love Mike for better or for worse. She did give him an ultimatum, however. She told him she wanted a separation until he decided to get help. This was mostly out of fear. She became afraid for her safety and the safety of their children, and decided that was where she would draw the line.

Martha took the children and moved out of the only home her children had ever known; they went to live with her sister. The children were now four and eight years old and they were very confused. With tears in his eyes, her eight-year-old son asked, "Why can't we go back home, mommy?" Martha felt heartbroken. "It is not safe at home right now," Martha explained. The children did not understand what was going on. Their lives had been turned upside down, and they kept asking why it was not safe to go back home. After three months, she decided it was time to get the children back to some semblance of normalcy. Martha returned home with the children, but now they were terrified of being in the house. She had to find a way to explain to them why home was safe now. But with Mike, nothing had changed. Still, Martha did nothing and said nothing. Thus, the silence continued.

The silence was not only about the assault, but about her life situation in general. During the years of silence Martha thought she had it all together; however, her reasoning was not as clear as she would have liked to think. She repressed all emotions, telling herself that she would be fine if her secrets remained in the past where they belonged. During that time, she had made some rash decisions, including the decision to marry someone with serious addiction issues, all the while keeping quiet about the things that were eating away at her. The silence about Mike's drug habit had damaging effects on her and on the family. She enabled Mike in many ways; but she felt she had to protect everyone else, even to her own detriment. Holding all of that inside took a deep toll on Martha. She felt the heavy burden of making things look normal on the outside while she suffered in silence. The silence about her family issues threatened to break her into pieces, but she persevered in the marriage nonetheless.

She knew the situation was far from ideal, but she was determined to provide some measure of stability for her children. She did not want them to feel the insecurity she felt as a child, and sacrificed her own happiness to make sure that never happened. She wanted financial security for them as well. They would not be tossed back and forth, not knowing where home would be from one day to the next. She reasoned that staying with their father would ensure that. So she remained silent; but as she started buckling under the strain some self-destructive tendencies began to surface.

Chapter 4

RECKLESS BEHAVIORS

SO HERE SHE was in a motel room that was in many ways reminiscent of the one where she had lost her virginity years earlier in such a cold and brutal manner. This time she had consented, but the outcome was much the same. A sense of emptiness pervaded her as she went through the motions without having a clear picture of the face above her.

Martha's reckless behaviors had started shortly after the assault, and the faces blended into each other after a while. Each time she would leave with the same sense of emptiness, and do it all over again another day. The first time after the assault, she found herself with a man whom she did not know was married at the time. He was very attractive, and at first, he kept it a secret that he was married. When the night came for the relationship to be consummated, he revealed his marital status. Of course, Martha refused to be with him and decided to walk away from the relationship. He said some very nasty things, and angrily accused her of not being 'normal' because she did not wish to continue in a relationship with him.

The next encounter was with a neighbor who also accused her of being 'abnormal' because she refused his advances. She flirted with him and allowed him to take certain liberties on occasion; not because she enjoyed it, but just maybe this time she might find pleasure. As time went by, she flirted with gangsters and drug dealers, and very nearly got herself into a few similar situations to the one that started this whole cycle. Keeping company with those characters was a product of her environment, as these were friends of older relatives and she was exposed to them as a result. She was protected from the worst of what could have been, however. Amidst all that, she had moved to another area again due to the financial difficulties at home. When she returned a year later she learned that several of the guys she and her sisters used to associate with had been killed. They were ambushed and killed in the same place – a house Martha used to visit frequently. Then there was the man she met online who told her she was beautiful. They communicated for a while, and the relationship was new and exciting while it lasted; but again, he remained just a name without a face.

Martha thought that marriage had put an end to that phase of her life, until 12 years into the marriage when she now found herself in this motel room. She was there for a one-night stand that would throw her already fractured marriage into another upheaval, and threaten to destroy the lives of others around her. Within weeks after Martha had returned home with the children, Mike agreed to leave and find a place to stay temporarily until they could work things out. Things went downhill very quickly after he moved out. She and Mike were still separated at the time, when she connected with an old flame from her childhood whom she had run into at a family function. Her decision to become intimately involved with this person was a calculated yet unsuccessful attempt to get Mike's attention. Immediately after the encounter, Martha cut off all communications with this person. Yet, she could not bear the thought of keeping a secret of that magnitude from Mike. She ended up confessing everything to him after the guilt weighed on her conscience for weeks.

Around the same time, an incident occurred at the hospital where Martha was employed. She was brutally attacked by a patient and suffered a severe back injury which put her out of work for a while. That, compounded with the other stressors in her life at the time, triggered severe panic attacks. She experienced chronic chest pains for about 6 consecutive months. When she got up in the mornings the pain was present, and it did not abate until she fell asleep again – if she was able to sleep at all. One day as she was eating dinner, the panic attack came on so suddenly her plate fell out of her hands and shattered on the floor in front of her. On another occasion, her neighbors called the ambulance and rushed her to the emergency room because she thought she was having a heart attack. It turned out there were no symptoms of heart problems despite the severe chest pains and shortness of breath. The doctor diagnosed it as a panic attack. Then another day she pulled off the highway on her way home from work as the chest pain, shortness of breath, confusion and disorientation began. She was in rush-hour traffic on the highway, and thought she was losing her mind. She rushed to the closest police department just to find safety. After calming herself, she recognized there was no physiological cause for her symptoms. Once again, this turned out to be classic symptoms of a panic attack.

Martha sought professional help for the anxiety by talking to a psychiatrist. She was prescribed medication for the anxiety symptoms, but she soon began to obsess about the possibility of becoming addicted to the medication. This brought on a bout of depression for which she was subsequently started on antidepressants. The antidepressants made her have what felt like an out of body experience, and within two weeks she decided to stop all the medication cold-turkey. However, she still felt stuck in a cycle of depression and anxiety, one compounding the other. The symptoms continued with no hope of abating, and Martha spiraled deeper into depression while she struggled to manage the finances.

As Martha became more and more depressed, she felt all alone in the Northeast where she had relocated right after the marriage. Her mother was living in the south at the time, but she took the time to speak to Martha on the phone daily, offering words of encouragement and songs of comfort. By now, the depression was so severe, that Martha had lost the desire to live. She packed her children up and sent them to stay with her sister in another state for what seemed like the longest three weeks of her life.

During the darkest hours, she would just cry constantly. She experienced a pervasive sense of sadness and hopelessness. She was unable to sleep at nights; she lost her appetite; and she lost all motivation and interest in anything pleasurable in life.

Having no desire to socialize, she withdrew from others and at times felt death would be welcome. She was anxious that she might hurt herself, but at the same time she did not want to die. She became terrified of being alone. She would look out the window at the sunshine and wonder why she was unable to feel happy. She would ask The Lord, *"How long will this go on?"* *"Why is it that everyone else around seems so content, yet I cannot find any pleasure in life?"* A few of her close friends made it their duty to take her along with them to their jobs, where she would sit and wait for them to finish working. It was as if she needed a babysitter. She felt like a burden to the people around her, and realized she could not go on this way. She needed this to end or it would surely be the end of her. It was at that point that she made up her mind to take her children back and fight for her life; but the gloom did not disappear overnight.

When Mike moved out, it was with the understanding that he would get treatment and one day be reunited with his family. Thus, Martha did not do anything right away; she was still hopeful that he would see the need to seek help even if his only motivation was to save his family. During that time, she and her family begged and pleaded with Mike to make the right decision and return home. However, he was not yet ready to give up his drug habit, and decided he would give up his family instead. Martha waited two years before finally working up the courage to file for a divorce. On the day the divorce became final, Mike told Martha he had changed his mind and wanted to work things out. But his habits had not changed and it had taken a great deal out of Martha emotionally just to get to that place. She had forgiven Mike, but she could not make herself go back into a situation that threatened to destroy her.

Chapter 5
THE SPIRITUAL JOURNEY

AS THE DEPRESSION wore on Martha would try to pray, but she could not see God's face. Sometimes, all she could say was "Jesus." She felt God had hidden His face from her. She felt lost in a black hole, unable to emerge into the light. She wondered how long the fog would last, but each day brought more of the same. She would look through the window on a sunny day, and wonder why everyone else in the world seemed happy while she could not find a reason to live. She would wake up on an overcast day and feel like she could not make it through the day. The fear that she would not make it through that ordeal was very real; then the anxiety started to become more generalized. She was afraid of being alone; afraid to be around knives or sharp objects; afraid she was going to hurt herself. She was afraid that she might hurt her children without really intending to.

Martha sought counsel from the pastor, who listened with kindness and compassion. He counseled her to confess to God who loved her enough to forgive her and restore her to a right relationship with Him. He shared that he felt she was abused in the marriage and abandoned, and reminded her that God wanted so much more for her. He told her God wanted *to prosper her and give her an expected end.* He reminded her that when God's people turned their backs on Him, he too divorced himself from them; thus, God understood what she was going through. This offered Martha a glimmer of hope, but she would not find her way out of the fog right away.

During the worst times, it was her belief in God that kept her sane. She read the Bible and prayed constantly, filling her mind with positive messages with every waking moment. To fill her empty hours, she started visiting the sick members of our church daily, including those confined to nursing homes. She started writing letters to inmates and often went into the prisons to visit young people who were locked away. Ministering to others brought Martha a great deal of comfort. It took her mind off her own problems as she focused on encouraging others. It also enlightened her when she recognized that others had greater challenges they were dealing with in their lives.

Still she needed the support of her family. She would sit on the phone with her mom for hours while her mom sang to her. Two of the hymns her mother would sing to her over the phone were: *God Will Take Care of You* and *Does Jesus Care.* She found much comfort in the words of those hymns, as well as in children's songs such as *Let the Sun Shine In.* She also found a great deal of strength in reading the Psalms. She always had to keep her mind occupied; otherwise, the negative thoughts would come and she would start to panic. She used this time to commune with God and beg Him for mercy and forgiveness. She was having a very difficult time forgiving herself even though she had asked Mike's forgiveness and he had eventually forgiven her. It was with a great deal of fasting and prayer that she was finally able to give her burdens to God.

Then she discovered a new favorite book, *The Desire of Ages* by E. G. White. She read it cover to cover several times, each time finding new meaning and much needed comfort. She fell in love with Jesus all over again every time she read this book. Then she was led to a self-help book entitled *An End to Panic: Breakthrough Techniques for Overcoming Panic Disorder* by Elke Zuercher-White. The road was a difficult one indeed, but she was determined to beat the anxiety and depression at all costs. As she prayed and worked on the self-help exercises suggested in the book, the anxiety symptoms slowly abated. The most effective techniques for Martha were the progressive relaxation exercises. She would focus on certain muscle groups starting at her neck and working down to her toes, and systematically tense and relax each muscle group until her entire body was relaxed. She also effectively used strategies of "thought blocking" and "thought stopping." When a negative thought of fear and anxiety began to surface, she would instantly stop the thought by repeating "STOP" in her mind, and immediately replace the thought with a pre-determined positive memory or image. Her favorite image was of being on the beach in Mexico, sitting in a hammock by the ocean and listening to the waves lapping against the shore. Then she started practicing the strategy of fixing her mind on a time in the future when things would be better. There were times when she could not even be sure of the next moment. But eventually, she could find hope in the next couple of hours, which soon became a full day. Soon she could string together a couple of good days in a row. However, it was approximately 18 months before the chest pains disappeared completely and she started to emerge from the depression. As time went by, Martha made steady progress toward healing; but she would continue to suffer from anxiety and insomnia for many years. She used sleep medications as needed during those years, but was careful not to use them so frequently that she might risk becoming dependent on them.

In a renewed relationship with God, Martha became more self-aware. She gradually regained her confidence, and with that came a renewed sense of self-worth. She began to see the reality of how this horrific experience had changed the course her life, and she made a conscious decision to put an end to the devastating effects. She came to recognize her value as a human being, and determined to stop behaving like a casualty. Instead, she came to see herself as a valuable person again, worthy of love and affection. She eventually became re-baptized and started out on a new page.

Martha's spiritual journey has spanned more than 35 years. She has come to know a forgiving God who exhibits unconditional love toward her despite her many faults. Serving God has now become a lifestyle for her. Regardless of the ups and downs, she remains true to her faith because she does not know what she would have done without God in her life to provide hope for a better future. Her faith has been instrumental in getting her through the most difficult times in her life, and she is confident in the fact that there is nothing that she is unable to conquer. Throughout the many challenges, she found amazing strength by tapping into her spirituality. However, the scars that remained would inform her choices in life for years to come.

Chapter 6

EFFECTS ON SELF-CONCEPT

SELF ESTEEM

LOADING...

MUCH OF THE agony Martha felt over the years was due to the pain that her loved ones suffered indirectly because of her experience. This goes not only for the night she was kidnapped, but also for the poor decisions she subsequently made that caused them pain. One of those choices was her decision to get involved in another relationship very shortly after her divorce from Mike. The divorce was finalized in 2004 and by 2005 she was dating Marvin. She was on the rebound but she did not know it at the time. She had cautions from her family, and she herself recognized certain warning signals that this was not the person for her. She ignored all the signs because she wanted so badly to restore the family unit. At 35 years of age she had never lived alone, because when she first got married it was straight out her mother's house.

Only one year after her first marriage ended, Martha started dating Marvin. After they had dated for three years, she and Marvin got married. Marvin told her at the outset that for him, marriage was nothing but a financial contract. He insisted that she signed a pre-nuptial agreement, which she later learned was a scam since her salary was four times that of his. She was so desperate to have companionship that she did not even read the agreement; she took his word that he was trying to protect a rental home he had acquired prior to the marriage so that he could pass it down to his children from prior relationships. She later learned that his was a scam: Marrying someone with considerably more asset under a prenuptial agreement; contributing minimally during the marriage; then taking her for half the assets amassed when the inevitable divorce takes place. During the marriage, Marvin refused to contribute to the finances. Martha saved emails and other correspondences where she communicated to Marvin the strain she was under as she struggled to manage the finances all by herself, while he invested all his resources into his rental property and his business.

The marriage started to fall apart within the first year when it became clear to Martha that there was no love involved. She found herself crying frequently due to the constant sadness. Marvin showed no affection toward her, and he made it clear that he did not love her children. The children could not walk freely in the house. If the floor boards squeaked when they walked around the house getting ready for school in the mornings, he would scream at the top of his lungs that they are making too much noise. That was a very sad time for the children. Marvin soon became verbally abusive, using profanity to her in the presence of the children. He never contributed financially to the home or to Martha's children from her first marriage, which she later learned was clearly stipulated in the pre-nuptial agreement.

Marvin did everything in his power to intimidate and belittle Martha, as if deliberately trying to destroy her self-esteem. He would insult and talk down to her, and withdraw from a casual touch if she reached out to him; he claimed that he was not raised to give or receive affection. Yet she remained in the marriage for three years. During that time, she craved Marvin's attention; she would go through an entire week sometimes without physical touch from another adult. This was a pathetic way to live when there was a spouse living in the same house. Marvin's excuse was that he did not grow up that way. He would only engage in intimate relations for his own pleasure when he had a desire. This did little for Martha's response to him, as there were no affectionate touches or kind words during the day that would put her in a frame of mind for intimacy at night. If she wanted to have a conversation with him he told her she had to make an appointment, and they could only have serious conversations on Thursday evenings. In hindsight, the whole situation was downright ridiculous.

When the relationship showed serious signs of deterioration, Martha became very concerned. She approached Marvin one Saturday, as this just could not wait until Thursday evening like he preferred. They were on their way back from a concert and she brought up the subject when they were almost home. "I have been very depressed lately because of the way things are at home; I think we should seek marital counseling from the pastor," she said to Marvin. "What can the pastor tell me that I don't already know?" said Marvin with an air of arrogance. "He may be able to give us some advice on how to handle some of the issues," Martha responded. "I don't need any counseling," said Marvin gruffly. "There's something wrong with you, so you go," he continued. By now they had pulled up in the driveway at home and Marvin shut off the engine. As they sat there in the car, Martha could not believe he was that egotistical. "You mean it doesn't matter to you if your marriage falls apart?" she asked incredulously. "I am like stone," he replied haughtily. "I don't feel anything."

Martha sought counseling for herself through the pastor. She shared with the pastor Marvin's attempts to control and belittle her, and to destroy her spirit. She shared the fact that he would not allow her to make any decisions in the home; he was the one who chose the color of the curtains and the type of furniture they bought with complete disregard for her opinion. Marvin told her what to eat, who to be friends with, and who not to talk to. He told her what to wear and how to do her hair, attempting to make her into someone she was not. He criticized her constantly, from the way she looked to the way she cooked.

He would try to intimidate her by sharing tales of his violent past, and then asking the rhetorical question: "You are scared of me, aren't you?" After sharing stories about how he had threatened and intimidated other women in his past, he would say to Martha, "I can tell you are nervous around me." That was his twisted objective, and he harped on it constantly. Martha had good reason to be afraid of Marvin. A few months before they got married, he was involved in an incident on the church property which resulted in him being charged with assault of a 17-year-old boy. That should have been deterrent enough for Martha; but she gave him the benefit of the doubt when he claimed the young man had attacked him first and that he had reacted instinctively, leaving evidence of bodily harm to the child. Because it was a first offence in that jurisdiction, he was able to make a deal that if he stayed out of trouble for 18 months the records would be sealed after that time. Martha supported him throughout that whole ordeal, yet he took pride in inflicting verbal and emotional abuse on her – his biggest supporter. He constantly put her down, and frequently told her she was *'unbalanced.'* He would use curse words to her that no decent person would even think to utter, and then go into the church and stand before the congregation as a leader. Martha remembered walking out of the church one day when she saw him leading out in the program, refusing to deal with the hypocrisy. A friend came outside to the parking lot and encouraged her to come back inside, reminding her that God can use imperfect persons to do His work.

Marvin continued to refuse marital counseling, and after unsuccessful efforts to bring healing to the marriage, Martha decided to file for a divorce. Again, Martha felt abandoned by her spouse, as he was the one who rejected her. The divorce was very ugly and distasteful, as Marvin spread horrible rumors about Martha's character to justify why his marriage ended. She had some good friends who knew her well enough to ignore his allegations, but others used this as an opportunity for gossip. Martha could hold her head high, however. She had a clear conscience because she never stooped to Marvin's level in this relationship. She never responded in kind to his abusive behavior; instead, she extricated herself from the situation as quickly as possible.

During the divorce proceedings, Marvin demanded that Martha reimburse him for his half of the deposit on the home they had purchased together only three years prior. They did an appraisal and it showed there was no equity in the house, so Martha told him she did not have that kind of money. He told her to withdraw the $10,000 from her retirement funds and give it to him, or he would not sign the divorce papers; but Martha insisted that she did not have it. Within a week of that conversation, Martha's house was burglarized. Someone smashed a window and broke into the house while they were out, leaving her and her children feeling awfully violated and afraid. The burglar did not touch any of her electronics and other valuables, but instead, was more interested in rifling through her financial documents. The perpetrator also took $400 in cash which her son had saved in his change jar, and turned her and her daughter's dresser drawer upside down on the floor. Martha told the police she suspected Marvin was the perpetrator. In a huge confrontation only a week prior, he had forced his way into the garage, leaving a footlong tear in the garage door panel. The police took fingerprints, and of course, Marvin's fingerprints were found on the smashed window. However, the police could not prove that he had broken in because he used to live there, and his fingerprints would be present everywhere anyway. Marvin denied the allegations; but shortly thereafter, he bragged about breaking into Martha's house to someone in his place of business. That person, who was a mutual acquaintance, came back and told Martha.

Martha ended up agreeing to give Marvin the $10,000 after he paced back and forth in the courthouse for about five hours on the day the divorce was to be finalized. An elder from the church pleaded with him to let it go, but he refused to budge until he was assured he would get the money. Marvin would end up taking an $1800 check from Martha's mailbox which was written to Martha "or" Marvin; it was a refund from the mortgage company for overpayment in the escrow account that year. He admitted to taking the money, though it belonged solely to Martha. Marvin had been out of the house for over a year, and he had not contributed to the mortgage during that time. Martha paid him the $10,000 minus the $1800.

Martha recognized that she had made a complete fool of herself by going against her family's wishes and marrying Marvin. Nevertheless, she sought the support of her mother and her sister, both of whom again stood by her without saying, *I told you so.* She admitted to herself and to her family that she had accepted far more disrespect and abuse than anyone should. Martha came to realize that this was all coming from Marvin's insecurities, as he had frequently expressed insecurities about the fact that Martha made more money than he did. Marvin ended up trampling on her to elevate himself and make himself feel like more of a man; but Martha's part in it was in accepting the mistreatment.

When this second marriage was over, Martha felt like she had again lost precious time, still seeking for that elusive thing called love. She admitted that this situation was a result of poor choices on her part regardless of the circumstances that led up to it. *But could the loving God she had come to know expect her to go through life without ever finding that love and companionship she so desired?* Despite the church's position on divorce, she felt she was the one who was abandoned on both occasions. At times she would question God: *Will I ever find true love?* God's response to her would be: *The kind of love you are seeking, you can find only in Me.* She discovered that only by relying on God can human beings even coming close to replicating to that type of love; but that lesson still took some time to sink in.

SHATTERED BUT SHELTERED

Chapter 7

EFFECTS ON LIFE GOALS AND SUBSEQUENT RELATIONSHIPS

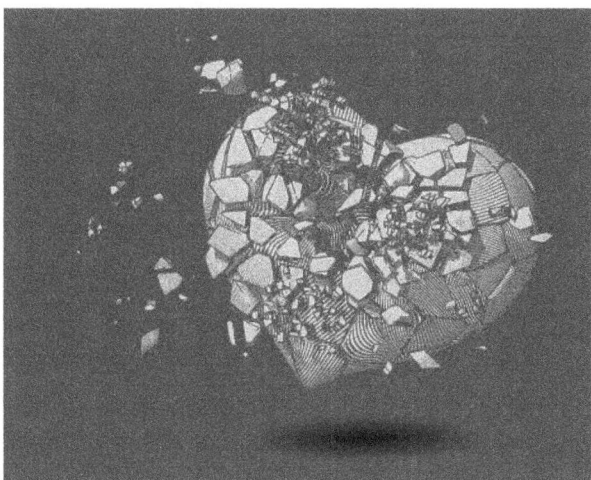

THE EMOTIONAL TRAUMA did not stop Martha from achieving her career goals. She would eventually complete her education and land a fulfilling job that allowed her to be financially secure in caring for her family as a single mother. She feels accomplished in many aspects of her life, and has now supported both her children through college as well. However, she made some poor choices along the way, leading to a lifetime of emotional pain, confusion and loneliness.

Martha had met her first husband when she was 18 years old, just two years after the assault. They were introduced by his mother, who was a dear family friend. Mike's mom was the type of person who would bring bags of groceries to Martha's mom when they were struggling financially. She would also offer Martha's family a ride to and from church whenever possible. When she and Mike were dating, Martha recalls regularly going with him and his mom to a shopping plaza in a poverty-stricken area where homeless men and women used to hang out on the streets. Mike's mother would load her car trunk with food for the homeless every Wednesday night. The usual fare was corned beef and cabbage with white rice. Mike and Martha would help to prepare the meals, and they would load his mother's white Toyota and drive to the plaza to feed the homeless. They were always there waiting because they knew they would have a hot meal on Wednesday nights. They would sing a song or two, pray with the men and women, then serve them from the trunk of the little car.

Mike and Martha had some good times together early on; but looking back now, she does not think either of them knew what love was at the time. Due to the emotional turmoil Martha was dealing with at the time, she made a very impulsive decision regarding marriage just three years into the relationship. Nevertheless, they both grew to love each other over time. Martha graduated from college and started working in a private practice owned by her former professor and mentor. Mike had relocated to the south to go to school, but he had enrolled part-time in college and dropped out. Mike and Martha decided to take a road trip to visit his family in the north who were running a family-owned heavy and highway construction business. Mike and his siblings all had shares in the company, but Mike was not able to contribute at the time because he was in school. He was the youngest of six children, and his family wanted to give him the best opportunity in life. If he had succeeded, Mike would have been the first in his family to graduate from college. However, this was not to be. His siblings were struggling to pay someone else as a laborer in his place. On this trip, Martha met the rest of Mike's family for the first time, and they welcomed her warmly. Seeing that he was no longer in school, he no longer had an excuse not to do his share in carrying the load at the company. His siblings then insisted that he returned to work in the family business, where they put tuns of steel into bridges and highways.

On the ride back, Mike and Martha discussed the fact that he would have to return home to work in the family business. On impulse, the two of them decided to get married so they would not have to be separated when he moved. They planned the wedding in six months and moved within two months of getting married. On a side note, Martha would come to learn 20 years later that many people in the church where she grew up assumed she was pregnant when she got married, hence the reason for her hasty departure. When she first went back home to visit with her son, friends would ask her son's age. When she told them his age, they would insist that he is a year older. She did not understand it at the time; but when she broached the subject with her sisters, they confirmed that there were rumors when she left.

When Mike and Martha settled in the north, the leaves where just changing colors as the Fall season was fast approaching. They lived with his family for six months while Martha searched for work. Soon she landed a job working for the state hospital, and they were able to move into their own place.

Mike was patient with Martha when she was unable to enjoy sexual intercourse. He understood the trauma she had experienced, and did everything he could to help her get through it. He later admitted to her however, that he had always felt she was 'damaged goods' because she had been raped. It hurt Martha deeply, but she could not even argue; at the time she had no defense. Mike had shared with her prior to their marriage that he had some issues with cocaine and marijuana use, but he said it was in the past. She would not know the extent of his addiction until after the marriage. She had selected someone with some serious issues that would have an indelible impact on her life for years to come; but she had her own issues after all.

She would end up working for the state for about nine years. During that time, there were many ups and downs in their marriage, but no one knew. Mike's drug habit had gotten the best of him, but Martha kept it private to make things look as normal as possible to anyone looking on. She did not speak of it to her family or to anyone else for that matter.

The ups and downs in life led to a delay in Martha accomplishing her career goals, however it did not stop her from achieving what she initially set out to do in life. After taking a year off to homeschool her children, she started focusing on her career. Her resume was posted online, but she was not actively looking for a job. Then a Canadian doctor from a local hospital contacted her out of the blue. He said he saw her resume, liked her background, and could use her skills. He described her as a sponge, soaking up all the information she came across.

For the next year she worked at the hospital, until a colleague offered her an opportunity to double her salary by working for a small private practice. Having been recently divorced and with only one salary now, she gladly took the opportunity and dealt with a three-hour morning commute for almost four years. After gaining some experience, she then took a small cut in salary to work closer to home in the same field. She worked at the new location for six years, while she returned to school to work on her doctorate. This position was a springboard which served to advance her career. She would eventually complete her doctorate, and start teaching part-time at a local college while she continued full-time in the practice. Her work was extremely rewarding, and she was at her best when engaged in the productive and meaningful activities of her day-to-day tasks.

Relationships had always been difficult for Martha to maintain, however. As a teenager, she had changed four different high schools in four years due to the instability at home; this made it difficult to form lasting friendships. Over the years, she found herself surrounded by many acquaintances, but only a few could be considered close friends. The same went for family relationships, as she had always found it difficult to reach out and connect with relatives. It was about four years after the divorce that she worked up the courage to share with her family what really took place in her first marriage. That was also when Mike's family learned of the extent of his drug addiction. Mike's late mother was initially disappointed, as she thought Martha was the one who had abandoned him. However, before her passing she would come to understand the issues Martha had dealt with for the 15 years she and Mike were together.

Despite everything, Martha finds it difficult to regret her relationship with Mike; after all, it produced two wonderful children. Parenting came easy for Martha. She dedicated her children to God at an early age, and asked God to protect them at all cost from the evils of the world. She also did her best to show them a good example in everything she did.

The responsibility she felt for raising them to become well-adjusted, God-fearing and productive citizens prompted her to keep them constantly in her prayers. She homeschooled them early on and instilled in them the values she had learned as a child. Homeschooling gave them a jump start, and by the time they went into the public-school system they were excelling academically. The divorce was extremely difficult on them, however. Her son was only ten years old at the time and was very close to his father. He was very distressed about the divorce. Martha had discussed with his teachers the situation at home, but her son's grades soon started slipping in school. Martha had to use some tough love to get him to snap out of the slump. At that time, she spoke with the teachers again and let them know there is to be no excuse for slipping grades. The expectation was that he would push through the difficult times and continue functioning despite the challenges. Her daughter who was six at the time, did not verbalize her feelings much; but Martha sought counseling for them both. She is thankful that they have made it through the worst by God's grace.

A few years ago, Martha saw a package come in the mail addressed to her son. It was a box containing their father's clothes and personal belongings sent from a state correctional facility. Martha informed Mike's sisters who frantically started making some calls; they did not know whether he was dead or alive. They were not able to confirm his whereabouts for several days; then finally they were told he was alive but incarcerated. Martha completed the necessary paperwork to be able to visit him. When his time had been served, Martha and her sister worked with Mike's family to get him released to a shelter.

Still, Mike's situation remains very precarious, as he is currently homeless. He sleeps in a shelter at nights, and if the shelters are full, he sleeps under a bridge. That is difficult for his children and loved ones to see. His family tried to help him on several occasions, and he would get back into the workforce with no trouble. Then he would turn his back on them as soon as he received his first paycheck and end up back on the streets. They connected him with the Veteran's Administration (VA) and informed them he served in the US Army and was honorably discharged. After verifying his service, the VA found him an apartment which they paid in full until he got on his feet. When he started working, the arrangement was that they would supplement by paying seventy percent and he would pay thirty percent. As soon as they got him established in the apartment and he started working, he found himself on the streets again, unable to handle his personal finances for more than a month. His drug habit continues to take every penny out of his pocket. On several occasions, he would ask family members to bank his money for him and help him to manage the finances. As soon as he gets the cravings, he comes knocking at their door in the middle of the night demanding his money.

Martha and her children remain prepared for any eventuality. They live with the possibility that Mike might be found dead one day from on overdose, or that drug dealers might take his life in exchange for money he owes them. After 25 years, he is still pawning off his belongings for a quick fix. As a result, he is not able to maintain the cell phone which the VA provided for him. When Martha hears from him these days, it is from a borrowed phone on which he cannot receive calls. About a year ago Martha's sister picked him up for his son's college graduation, and she had to pick him up from the side of the road. It was always necessary to bring him a change of clothes. He changed in a public bathroom and cleaned up enough to attend the graduation. There was a celebration dinner with family and friends, and at the end of the day they dropped him off on the side of the road again, as he had no place to call home.

The children are now adults and they still love their father dearly, as Martha has never said anything negative to them about him. They eventually discovered his issues for themselves as they got older, but they still respect him as their father. His son has distanced himself from him somewhat, which is probably his way of dealing with the pain. Martha continues to do whatever she can for Mike, however. She can never see him go hungry if she has the opportunity to help. She shows kindness to Mike, not only because of the kindness his mother showed to her family when they were in need, but also because of the kindness Mike has in his heart for others. On separate occasions, Mike had allowed Martha to accept into their home four different families who were in need. Mike had welcomed these families into his home, and each family stayed with them for an average of about 6 months until they could stand on their own financially. So even though Mike struggled with the torment of drug addiction, he had a gift for helping others, which was also a legacy of his late mother. Martha and her children still maintain a very close relationship with Mike's family; what happened between her and Mike did not disrupt that relationship.

Chapter 8
DEALING WITH THE FALLOUT
30 YEARS LATER

IN 2017, MARTHA spoke of the assault in a public forum for the first time since that fateful night 30 years ago. The first attempt to verbalize the experience during her Master's program was unsuccessful, and was only in a one-on-one setting with a classmate she was role-playing with. This time, however, she gave a testimony in front of an audience of friends, family members, and church members during a youth program dealing with mental health. Most of her family members would learn of Martha's experience for the first time. It was not an easy decision for Martha to make even then. She and Eve prepared some Power Point slides for a talk on mental health, and

Martha's testimony was to be incorporated into that presentation. She prepared for the presentation for months, but it was only the night before that she made the final decision to share her story. At that point she felt she had nothing to lose, and others had much to gain.

As Martha stood in front of the audience – many of whom had known her since childhood – she did not know what she would say. She did not feel a rehearsal was necessary, so she simply spoke from the heart. "If you think that depression only affects certain people, think again," she began. "I have also suffered from depression." The room went so silent, you could hear a pin drop. As Martha recounted the events of the assault, she prayed for strength to hold it together. She became almost tearful at times, but Eve was right there as she had always been when Martha needed support. As she described the events leading up to the divorce and how depression and anxiety came to a climax, she felt bolstered by the response she was receiving from the audience.

At the end of the presentation, a few of the audience members started to approach Martha one by one. She received supportive comments from a few of her friends, and others just hugged her. Some simply squeezed her hand and kept going. Others, including some of her family members, chose to avoid the subject altogether, refusing to bring it up. Martha finds that people often do not know how to broach the subject; and frankly, they probably do not know what to say to her about it. She is guessing that people probably avoid the conversation because they are afraid that a reminder of the incident will be too painful for her. The truth of the matter is, Martha does not mind talking openly about her experience.

After the presentation, one of her good friends asked her some pointed questions about the incident, which she did not mind going into in more detail about. One of her aunts also brought up the subject, as she recalled asking Martha when she showed up the morning following the assault, "Why are you so dirty?" This was a conversation Martha had effectively blocked out of her memory for thirty years. It only came back to her when her aunt mentioned it after the presentation. Martha's aunt admitted that at the time, she thought Martha's account of the rape was only a dramatic excuse for staying out all night. That is an extremely painful thing for Martha to come to terms with. The few people who knew about the incident – from the police officer to Martha's family members – just saw her as a rebellious teenager who got in over her head because of poor choices. The fact remains, Martha did not choose that by any measure.

Out of an audience of approximately 200 people, only about five persons brought up the subject with Martha in a meaningful conversation. Martha appreciated all the gestures of encouragement, but she was happy to interact with those who engaged her more deeply on the issue. One friend felt comfortable enough to share with her that his daughter had a similar experience. What Martha wanted to say to him but did not say was: *Be patient with your daughter if she should make some poor choices. An experience such as this creates in her a desire for things she has no business desiring. It grows out of a need for genuine love…an attempt to associate love with the sexual act…to have confirmation that she is normal.* Another friend and mentor shared with Martha how blessed he was by the testimonial, and felt comfortable enough to share with her some of his own personal challenges. It warmed her heart to know that people did not judge her, but instead offered support. She somehow felt the support even from those who were not able to openly discuss the issue with her.

It was a few months after that presentation when Martha brought up the subject with her mother once more. Martha had tried to bring it up even before the presentation, but her mom became very defensive and they were not able to finish the conversation. This time, they talked openly about the incident after 30 long years, and Martha's mom expressed how sorry she was that Martha had to endure such pain. This was a very cathartic experience for both Martha and her mom. Martha assured her mom that she had worked through the issues and did not harbor any anger and resentment. Martha's mom expressed to her how proud she was of her strength and resilience, and her courage in being able to share her story in that forum. It liberated them both in a sense from feelings of shame, and allowed Martha to release her mom from guilt.

Shortly thereafter, Martha decided she no longer wished to continue in a long-term relationship she had been involved in. She had been seeing Josh for almost five years, and was hopeful that the relationship would someday lead to marriage. For a good portion of this relationship, Josh hid Martha from his friends and family. He did not introduce her to his family until about two years into the relationship, and very few of their mutual friends knew they were dating until three years in. He did not make any connections to her on social media, and seldom attended church with her. His reason for this was that he was a very private person and did not want everyone into his business. In the five years they were together, they were seldom seen together in public, and never attended social functions together. This left Martha feeling lonely and neglected as she continued to attend church functions and social events alone. This was very reminiscent of her two previous relationships, though each was for very different reasons. She felt unfulfilled in the relationship, and still yearned for companionship. This led her to do some deep introspection. Knowing that she was beautiful, intelligent, and accomplished in life, she began to question whether she was asking for too much out of a relationship, or if she was just selecting the same type every time to fill a specific need. She concluded it must be the latter, as she could not imagine that all relationships were that lacking in fulfillment. Still, she persevered in the relationship, hoping for a future with Josh. They had several conversations about marriage, and Josh led Martha to think they were on the same page; but he kept putting it off each year. He offered what Martha saw as one excuse after the other, ranging from family obligations to personal things he would like to accomplish first. The conversations always ended with Martha apologizing for being selfish enough to suggest that they should move on with their lives when he had so many personal commitments.

Martha sensed that Josh was either not ready to commit to her, or he did not see in her what he was looking for in a wife. Yet out of her love for him and a desire for companionship, she remained in the relationship even when it became clear they had very different goals. Soon her desire for marriage started to wane, however. She felt that even if Josh were to propose, it would only lead to resentment on his part if he felt pressured into making the decision. She came to realize that she did not need someone who was not able to prioritize her in his life. She started feeling stifled, as if she was being held hostage in a relationship with no potential for a future. She had spent the better part of her forties in this relationship where there was no chance of commitment.

She felt that somehow, she was missing out on the opportunity to meet someone who really cared about her enough to want to spend a lifetime with her.

Martha broached the subject with Josh one evening when she gave him a ride home from work. His car was out of commission, and they were sharing a vehicle. As she pulled up in his driveway she said to Josh, "We need to talk." Josh was somewhat taken aback; "It sounds serious," he said. "What's on your mind?" Martha shared with Josh that she wanted to end the relationship, citing his lack of commitment as an indication that the relationship was not important to him. His response was, "Well, I guess there is nothing I can say, you have made up your mind." "Try me," she said. "Tell me something that might help to change my mind." "No," Josh responded, "I am not going to do that; marriage is a priority for you, it is not a priority for me." In a mocking tone he continued, "I hope you find someone to marry you next year." It took only 15 minutes to discuss the termination of a 5-year relationship. That confirmed for Martha that she had done the right thing by ending the relationship. She felt that by selecting someone who was unavailable, she had again made a choice that was not good for her out of a desperate need for companionship, thereby subjecting herself to a very familiar pattern of mistreatment.

Against her better judgment, Martha kept second-guessing herself for months after the relationship ended. She had a great deal of conflicting feelings about whether she had done the right thing. Deep down she knew that the ball was never in her court. Yet, within three months she had gone back into the relationship, with Josh promising marriage in the coming year. He then changed his tune again on the first day of the new year, saying maybe he could see them being engaged by the end of the year. That is when Martha finally came to accept that Josh was only stringing her along, and marriage was never going to become a reality. Martha broke off the relationship once again, knowing that her decision would be final this time. "What's your hurry?" Josh asked. Martha reminded him that at that stage in their lives, dating for five years was not exactly hurrying. He became angry that she had the nerve to end the relationship, telling her that there were so many other women who wanted to marry him. He then mocked her once again by saying, "I hope you find someone who will marry you this year." In Martha's mind, she equated marriage with unconditional love and acceptance. Therefore, she felt justified in ending that relationship, as marriage without love and acceptance would mean nothing to her at any rate. She felt she had done the right thing by separating herself from an unhealthy situation.

In the end, Josh threatened that if he ever saw her talking to anyone else, he would smear her character so that no one else would ever want her. That was an enormously disappointing end to a relationship which Martha really thought was genuine, not to mention the hypocrisy of it. She truly loved Josh, and despite his lack of commitment, she had remained hopeful that this love would be reciprocated. This is a man she had affirmed and treated with such high regard, to the point where he started telling her frequently how lucky she was to be with him because he was so highly respected. However, their last exchange revealed that the mutual love and acceptance she constantly sought would continue to elude her. It did not shake her faith in God, however. She was reminded once again that the kind of unconditional love she sought could not be found in humans unless they were willing to submit to a higher power. This relationship was, nevertheless, a learning experience which served to further bolster Martha's courage, and strengthen her resolve to keep on persevering despite the obstacles.

Epilogue

THE QUESTIONS THAT Martha now asks herself are varied: *What have I gained from my life's experiences? What was the purpose of such a horrific, traumatic encounter early in life?* Martha admits she has gained inner strength from having gone through those experiences, and has developed into a more complete person. She has come to discover that entering a relationship spiritually and emotionally whole is the best thing she can do for herself and for any union. She and Eve remained inseparable over the years, but in recent years she has fostered a stronger relationship with Connie. Her relationship with Grayson remains distant, but that is mainly due to a lack of proximity.

Martha values relationships. Now it is her greatest joy to return to the little community in Baker's Town and spend time with the awesome friends she had formed such close connections with. She no longer looks to someone else to make her happy, but instead, selflessly seeks to contribute to a relationship in substantive and meaningful ways. She has learned that intimacy is a wonderful thing whenever it is within the right context; it involves caring about the things the other person cares about, and sharing each other's hopes and dreams. She has come to a place where she is content to be alone and not be lonely. From her many years of tarrying in stagnant relationships, she has learned that she is stronger than she has been portraying and deserves better than she has been accepting.

Her will to survive counts for something; but she does not take all the credit for the fact that her mind and body remain intact throughout the abuse she has endured. She feels it is in large part due to her faith in God and her drive to survive that she did not inadvertently self-destruct. Even though she was shattered by the assault, she was sheltered from disease and destruction, and from any incapacitating emotional damage. Furthermore, Martha feels protected from anger, resentment and bitterness in the aftermath, and grateful for the ability to forgive herself and others who have caused her pain. She never blamed her mother for how she handled the situation. At the time of the assault, her mom did the best she could under the circumstances. She remained calm and handled it the best way she knew how. Years later during Martha's struggle with depression, her mom was there for her again. Martha will be forever grateful for her mom's unwavering love and support, and for her constant encouragement and affirmation. Their mom had seen the potential in both her and Eve and enrolled them in the local college; whereas their dad had told Eve he was not going to waste his money sending her to college because she quits everything she starts. Martha's relationship with her father and stepmother has improved greatly over the years. She has never brought up the subject of her childhood with them; however, she has let go of the hurt, and the relationship she now seeks to foster with each of them is still a work in progress. When she became an adult, she simply refused to address her father at all, because it felt unnatural for her to call him 'Uncle Alan.' Thus, she would often refer to him as 'my father.' To this day, Martha still finds it very uncomfortable calling her father 'Dad,' but she does so on occasion.

Amidst all the ups and downs, Martha was sheltered and protected by a power greater than herself. All her searching led her to a deeper spiritual connection; and in finding God, she found peace. She is now at a point in her life where not much can rattle her. She has come to accept that none of her experiences were by chance. They may not have been God's plan for her life; but her experiences fortified her for subsequent trials, increased her faith, and ultimately led to the realization of her life's purpose which involves helping others to develop resilience when faced with adversity. She took the long road home to learn lessons that could have been more easily learned. Through it all, she has learned to let go of the hurt, and instead, use her experience to strengthen others. What it comes down to is a single-minded drive to keep on hurdling the obstacles, and a resolute determination to make it through the rough patches against all odds. Martha now lives in a constant state of thankfulness; she is thankful for her trials, and for the unwavering support of her family and close friends. She is thankful for the good times and the bad, because all these experiences converge to shape her character and mold her into the woman she is today.

If Martha's story can reach someone on the verge of falling into the trap that ensnared her, she will consider all her experiences to have been worthwhile. She will consider this recompense enough for having had to endure such pain. However, this would only be a partial fulfillment of what she now sees as her moral duty. She has come to recognize that the essence of self-fulfillment is often realized in giving back.

PART TWO
RESEARCH ON
SEXUAL ASSAULT

Chapter 9
SEXUAL ASSAULT ON COLLEGE CAMPUSES

RAPE IS A major social problem due to its prevalence in society and its effects on victims (Girelli, Resick, Marhoefer-Dvorak & Hutter, 1986). These researchers found that one in four women will be raped during their lifetime, and 20-30% of girls now age 12 will suffer a violent sexual assault. Sexual assault on college campuses is a serious societal problem with far-reaching consequences for victims. The literature shows that over a short 10-week period, between 11% and 28% of college women report some form of undesirable sexual experience ranging from unwanted sexual contact to rape (Orchowski & Gidycz, 2015). Yet few women report the incidences to the police or to campus authorities. According to the authors, only 8% of victims file a formal report, while 86% of victims report the incidence to a female peer. This may be due in part to the varied reactions women receive when disclosure is made.

Orchowski and Gidycz (2015) conducted further study of the levels of psychological symptoms associated with positive and negative reactions to sexual assault disclosure. Included in the study were 134 college women. Thirty-five percent of these women reported unwanted sexual experiences since the age of 14. To break it down further, "15% reported unwanted sexual contact; 2.9% reported sexual coercion; 9.6% reported attempted rape; and 8.3% reported completed rape (Lindsay & Gidycz, 2015). According to this study, 97% of assaults were perpetrated by someone the victims knew, and in 63% of the cases, the perpetrator was under the influence of an illicit substance. The women reported both positive and negative reactions to disclosure of sexual assault. The statistics above are supported by Ullman, Filipas & Townsend (2005) of the University of Illinois, who conducted a study of 1,084 women age 18 or older who had experienced sexual assault since age 14. They reported that 79.6% of the women were assaulted by someone they knew, while 20.4% were assaulted by strangers. More than 30% of the women and 60% of the attackers were using substances during the time of the assault; more than 20% said their attacker used physical force; and 17% of the attackers had weapons. About 50% of the women felt their lives were in danger; 60% actively resisted, yet approximately 87% suffered physical injury nonetheless (mostly minor). In addition, 70% of the women met criteria for Post-Traumatic Stress Disorder (PTSD), and 27% reported they had attempted suicide at some point in their lives. The women's average self-blame score was three times the norm, suggesting that they strongly blamed their own character and behavior for the assault. Of note is the fact that 80% of the women in this study disclosed their sexual assault to someone.

Some studies show that women who receive positive social reaction to disclosure are more likely to adjust well, while other studies show no significant relationship between positive social reaction and adjustment. Negative reactions, on the other hand may have more damaging consequences. Lindsay and Gidycz (2015), cite several studies which found that "negative social reactions are associated with higher levels of anxiety, depression, PTSD and problem drinking" (p. 3). In addition, women who received negative feedback following disclosure demonstrated higher levels of interpersonal sensitivity, hostility, phobic anxiety and paranoia. They hypothesized that this is probably because disclosure is usually made to family and friends, and negative reactions from such close acquaintances are usually unanticipated. Social reactions to disclosure have also been found to influence women's views of why sexual assault occur. Those who receive negative reactions generally give credence to the idea that sexual assault occurs because of the victim's behavior, and not due to the perpetrator, society, or by chance. Thus, self-blame and subsequent guilt can become a significant factor.

Ullman et al (2005) also corroborate the above findings, reporting that female victims of violent crimes receive less social support than do male victims, and crimes of sexual assault are no different. Women who disclosed the assault were asked to complete a Social Reactions Questionnaire (SRQ). Women received more negative reactions from their social support systems for disclosures of sexual crimes than they did for disclosures of other violent crimes. Thus, the decision regarding whom to disclose sexual assault to often has great consequences for women.

Ullman et al (2005) found that the type of support system women disclosed to – whether formal or informal sources – often determined the reactions they received. However, the factors that determine why women disclose to one type of support as opposed to the other have not been adequately explored in the literature. Informal support included romantic partners, parents, family members and friends. Formal sources included clergy, police, medical personnel, mental health professionals, and rape crisis counselors. Approximately two-thirds of victims disclose their assault, with 59% disclosing to informal sources and 41% disclosing to formal sources. Informal sources tend to provide emotional support, while formal sources tend to provide resources for injuries and psychological consequences such as depression and PTSD. Women tend to disclose the incident to formal sources when the circumstances conform to society's stereotypical definition of what a legitimate rape is – stranger rape for instance. Demographic factors such as the race of the victim and the offender play an important role in determining how an incident is defined, and subsequently, who the victim discloses to. It is not inconceivable then, that women often report sexual assault when they feel they will be believed, and to sources who will believe them. On the other hand, it appears that negative reactions might be related to greater risk of psychological consequences in victims of sexual assault.

According to Ullman et al (2005), the way women attribute blame and cope with the assault may also affect the choices they make regarding disclosure. Those who tend to blame themselves for the assault are less likely to disclose, and vice versa. The flip side is also true; the disclosures women make depend on the type of support she receives immediately following the incident. Those who received a greater number of negative social reactions were more likely to disclose to formal support sources. Those who received negative social reactions were also at a greater risk for symptoms of post-traumatic stress.

Martha was aware that based on the religious culture in which she grew up, people in her circles were very unlikely to look upon the assault incident objectively. Many in the church were quick to be judgmental when others did not measure up to their standards. This contributed to the many years of silence, as she had tremendous anxiety about disclosure among her family and acquaintances. She did not trust that she would receive the social support she needed. She felt they were more likely to blame her for placing herself in that position, so she kept it to herself to her great detriment.

The research shows that Martha's experience is not as isolated as one might think; however, females are not the only ones affected by sexual assault. According to RAINN (2018), the largest anti-sexual violence organization in the United States, male victims account for about 10 percent of all attempted or completed rapes. Their latest statistics show that about 2.7 million American males have experienced an attempted or completed rape. They also found that transgender college students were at a higher risk of sexual violence. It is interesting to note that male college students between 18-24 years of age were five times more likely to be victims of rape than non-college students of the same age.

This trend is seen across cultural lines as well. A 10-year study conducted at a Sexual Assault Center in Denmark found that of 55 male victims who came into the center, 53% were between the ages of 15 and 24. Male victims accounted for only 2% of total visits to the center over that time, however (Larsen & Hilden, 2016). Around 39% of these young men were students when the assault took place. In all cases, the perpetrator was male, and 68% of the victims reported themselves as heterosexuals. According to this study, male victims were more likely than females to be assaulted by a stranger and by more than one perpetrator. They claim that male victims were less likely to report the incident to the police – with only 42% reporting the assault in this case – and that under-reporting may be a bigger issue for males than it is for females who report at a rate of about 70%. The most common reasons males gave for not reporting the incident were: Feelings of guilt, uncertainty about the details, and wanting to forget.

Victims who do report the assault are often blamed for not coming forward soon enough, but from the literature one can conclude that in some cases there are compelling reasons for this delay. The shock of the experience itself was enough to paralyze Martha, rendering her immobile in the immediate aftermath. The guilt and shame that followed closely on the heels of this paralysis dictated that she remained silent, or risk paying the terrible consequences of disgrace and humiliation. In the silence, Martha avoided confronting the emotions at a time when the wounds were raw. Her silence may have protected her emotionally at a time when she was not able to deal with those feelings. However, she would soon enough come face-to-face with the reality of what had happened and experience the emotional impact.

Sexual assault on college campuses is all too common among both male and female students who are on the brink of

SHATTERED BUT SHELTERED

a new chapter in their lives. This new chapter can be derailed by an experience such as this, and for some, their very story may even be cut short. However, the outcome is determined by the actual impact the experience of sexual assault has on the life of the victim.

Chapter 10

THE PSYCHOLOGICAL IMPACT
OF SEXUAL ASSAULT

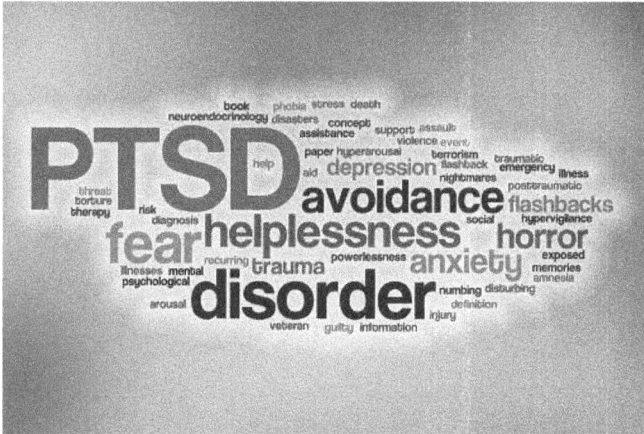

THERE ARE SERIOUS psychological consequences associated with sexual assault, ranging from anxiety and depression to PTSD and substance abuse (Ullman et al, 2015). Negative social reactions to disclosures of sexual assault was found to be linked to greater risk of PTSD in female victims of sexual assault crimes. Since those who experienced more stereotypical type incidents were more likely to disclose to both formal and informal sources, this liberal approach to disclosure led to more help-seeking among these women. They were less likely to blame themselves, and more likely to seek support and receive help in coping.

Other experts have confirmed that sexual assault before the age of 18 has long-term psychological consequences for victims (Hill, Kaplan, French & Johnson, 2010). These researchers went a step further than other researchers by investigating the factors that can mediate and potentially minimize such consequences. From a study of 2,402 predominantly Black and Hispanic low-income women with children in the Boston, Chicago, and San Antonio areas, they predicted psychological distress in adulthood among women who became victims of sexual assault before age 18. They concluded that overriding factors including emotional support and self-esteem could minimize the psychological effects of sexual assault and sexual coercion.

Martha did not give herself the benefit of emotional support due to her silence. By keeping the assault secret from her family and friends, she effectively shut down those avenues of support, thereby perpetuating and exacerbating the psychological effects. She may not have been lacking in self-esteem prior to the incident, but esteem issues certainly became a factor afterwards. The fact that she felt justified in remaining in abusive relationships is at least partially due to her lowered sense of self-esteem, granted that her upbringing likely contributed to those decisions as well. Regardless of her reason for tolerating disrespect and ill-treatment in those relationships, there is no doubt that she had some adjustment issues due to the assault.

Girelli, Resick, Marhoefer-Dvorak & Hutter (1986) found that rape has major and lasting effects for women with respect to several areas of adjustment. In a study of 41 women over the age of 18 who became victims of sexual assault before the age of 18, victims reported decreased sexual satisfaction for years following the incident. In addition, victims were more depressed than non-victims up to a year following the assault, and their views of fear were significantly affected for many years post-assault. These researchers claim that increased fear among victims of rape is not surprising considering the threat of injury or death that most victims experience during the incident. Overall, victims were found to experience more fear than non-victims, however the type and duration of fear varied. For six months to a year, victims experienced more fear than non-victims in rape-related fears. These included classical fears such as darkness; fear of failure or self-esteem fears; and other interpersonal fears. More importantly, however, is that a significantly greater number of victims experienced more tension than non-victims 16 years post assault. They found that while depression and social adjustment resolved within four months of the assault, fear and anxiety remained elevated for up to four years post-assault and often never returned to pre-assault levels.

Martha's case is very consistent with the findings in this report as it relates to fear response and other psychological distress. The defense mechanism which allowed her to shut down her emotions following the incident protected her from depression in the immediate aftermath. However, the anxiety manifested immediately following the assault and was perpetuated for years afterward. She also suffered from insomnia, which is still a struggle for her. She did end up dealing with depression years later when things came to a head. Even though the depression was triggered by other life circumstances, it was probably compounded by the many years of silence around the assault, and by the many years of abuse she endured in her first marriage. Her reaction to the break-up of her marriage was likely a reaction to all the losses she had suffered over the years, which she had never grieved for. In fact, she never had a typical reaction to the assault at the time of the incident, but her response to the incident much later in life was extreme.

There seems to be a link between the physical violence of an assault and the intensity of crisis reactions in women. Girelli et al (1986) cited a study of 27 victims one to sixteen years post-assault, which explored symptomology at various stages of recovery. They found that symptomology was affected by three main variables: Whether rape was completed; whether one or more assailants were involved; and whether the victim's life was threatened. Women who experienced more brutal rapes reported more intense fears and greater avoidance behaviors than women who had less brutal experiences. However, there was not a strong relationship between the extent and duration of violence and women's reaction. This sheds light on the possibility that the actual violence of an attack might be less influential on victims' reactions than the perceived threat. Higher levels of distress lead to greater debilitation among victims, however subjective distress cannot be clearly predicted by the actual level of violence in an assault experience.

For Martha, the perceived threat of violence apparently had significant impact on her response to the assault. She truly felt her life was threatened, which likely contributed to her extreme reaction. However, her childhood experiences may also have contributed greatly to her response as well, considering that she had deep-seated issues around feelings of physical safety and security. Her need for self-preservation became paramount during the assault; yet she lay there helplessly in that motel room that night. This created in Martha a great deal of inner conflict and psychological distress.

Stepakoff (1998) conducted a study on the effects of sexual victimization on suicidal ideation and behavior in U.S. college women. The study included 393 undergraduate women who completed self-report measures of their experiences surrounding sexual assault, as well as their experiences of hopelessness, suicidal ideation, and suicidal behaviors. According to this study, approximately 22-27% of female college students have been raped, and victims of sexual assault are at greater risk for suicidality than non-victims. They found that, overall, women had higher rates of suicidal ideation and suicidal behavior than men. Adult sexual assault among women was a strong predictor of current hopelessness and suicidal ideation; however, childhood sexual assault did not predict suicidal ideation. Instead, both adult sexual assault and childhood sexual assault strongly predicted suicidal behavior. This study reported that 1 in 4 rape victims had engaged in some type of suicidal behavior in contrast to 1 in 20 non-victims. Furthermore, women who experienced actual vaginal penetration with the use of physical force were more likely to engage in suicidal behavior than women who experienced penetration without the use of force and/or force without penetration.

One report showed that 70% of sexual assault victims experienced distress, but the researchers made no distinction between males and females when it came to psychological impact (RAINN, 2018). On the other hand, Mezey and King (1992) found that in some regions outside the U.S., sexual assault on men is taken less seriously even though males suffer serious psychological consequences as well. Sexual violence threatens the physical and emotional wellbeing of males as it does females; however, males have very different experiences and very different responses to the assault. Yet, the research on the prevalence, characteristics and sequelae of sexual assault among males is very limited. Rates of abuse among boys is still unclear, and is very likely due to under-reporting.

Larsen and Hilden (2016) suggest that most incidents of assault against males are perpetrated by males. They claim that being assaulted by someone of the same sex can activate questions in the minds of victims about their own sexuality. Among male perpetrators of sexual violence against males, power, control and revenge were more important than sexual gratification. Yet, male victims can experience involuntary erections during the assault, which may lead to increased trauma relating to thoughts about their sexuality, as well as feelings of guilt. The distress is not so much due to sexual orientation or how one identifies, but more so from the conflict in the minds of these men surrounding that. They also found that male victims – who were more likely than females to be intoxicated – waited longer than female victims to seek help for the assault. This could probably be due to a state of shock or being partially intoxicated immediately after the incident.

Regardless of the circumstances, it is extremely important that victims seek treatment following sexual assault. Immediate intervention can help victims to process what took place, but long-term therapy can help survivors manage the more perpetual consequences such as PTSD. Not only was Martha at risk for severe psychological consequences, but she suffered much of the emotional impact of the assault. In her case, these included decreased sexual satisfaction, and intense fears for an extended period which manifested into anxiety disorders and panic attacks. Yet, her experience is proof that intervening factors such as professional therapy and family support can override the impact of sexual assault and help the survivor navigate a path to positive adjustment. While this is true, there are certain self-destructive tendencies that many survivors of sexual assault will struggle to escape for years down the road.

Chapter 11

SELF-DESTRUCTIVE BEHAVIOR
– A CONSEQUENCE

RESEARCH SHOWS THAT individuals with a history of sexual abuse or assault are likely to engage in risky sexual behaviors and self-destructive behaviors (Green, Krupnick, Stockton & Goodman, 2005). To account for other factors or events in the person's history that may point to occurrences of risky behavior, Green et al studied 363 college sophomores, assigned to either a no-trauma comparison group or one of five assault groups: A single traumatic loss; a single physical assault; a single sexual assault; ongoing sexual or physical abuse; or multiple single traumas. Of the 363 participants, 209 experienced a traumatic event after the age of 12. They found that risky sexual behavior and suicidal ideation were most prevalent among women who had ongoing exposure to abuse; however, those who experienced a single violent attack were also more likely than those in the non-trauma group to engage in risky behaviors including risky sexual behaviors, suicidal behaviors, and violence perpetration.

Green et al (2005) cited multiple studies which showed that individuals who had exposure to forced sex engaged in their first voluntary sexual intercourse at an earlier age. They also found that women with a history of sexual abuse were more concerned about HIV infection. Women in the abuse group reported a greater number of sexual partners over a lifetime than women in the no-assault group, and a greater incidence of having sexual intercourse upon the first meeting. Women in the assault group also had higher rates of pregnancies, abortions, sexually transmitted diseases and being tested for HIV. Major depressive Disorder (MDD) and post-traumatic stress disorder (PTSD) were also found to increase the likelihood of high-risk behaviors. They found a significant correlation between PTSD and having been pregnant, having abortions, and having had STDs. PTSD was also associated with having suicidal ideations, suicide attempts, and dangerous sexual behaviors; while a lifetime history of major depressive disorder (MDD) was associated with number of pregnancies, lifetime number of sexual partners, and sex at first meeting.

Peters and Range (1996) also found that "Women who

were sexually abused as children often experience self-blame and self-destructive behaviors as adults..." (p. 19). The study reports that women who strongly blamed themselves for the assault were more severely depressed and suicidal, were more likely to have engaged in self-mutilation, and overall, had weaker coping skills than did low self-blamers. High self-blamers also had greater fear of suicide and greater fear of social disapproval than low self-blamers.

Related to guilt and self-blame is a tendency for childhood sexual assault victims to engage in risky sexual behaviors throughout adolescence and into adulthood. Ullman and Vasquez (2015) report a correlation between child sexual abuse and sexual assault revictimization in women. They claim children who have been victims of sexual abuse are twice as likely as non-victims to experience sexual assault in adolescence or adulthood. They also found that child sexual abuse victims engage in more risky behaviors as adults. They usually have a greater number of sexual partners; are more likely to exchange sex for money; are more likely to use drugs or alcohol prior to sex; and are less likely to use condoms. These factors set the stage for greater risk of revictimization. Wright, Friedrich, Cinq-Mars, Cyr, & McDuff (2004) also found a strong correlation between delinquency and self-blame for childhood sexual abuse. In addition, they found that violence during the abuse, depression, and lower quality mother-daughter relationships, were strongly linked to self-destructive behaviors.

Martha's experiences resonate in many ways with the experiences of those in the above studies. She developed an obsessive need to be tested for HIV infection, testing after every partner for years following the incident. Thankfully the results were always negative, but the fears were so intense that she was forced to develop a way to cope. She was at high risk for being revictimized as an adult as well, due to her indiscriminate sexual behaviors from adolescence through young adulthood. She was singularly determined to discover the pleasures that she was taught to expect from the sexual encounter, but which she was clearly cheated out of due to that horrible experience. That led to decisions that placed her at risk for being revictimized.

The long-term consequences of sexual abuse are staggering. Green et al (2005) found that victims of childhood sexual abuse were twice as likely than non-victims to drop out of college after the first semester, and those with PTSD were more likely to drop out. Clinical intervention is needed to prevent occurrences such as these. Intervention programs may be most effective when they begin in junior high school or high school; however, beginning in college might still be useful. These programs could provide the structure and support necessary to build coping skills.

Martha was not able to escape the self-destructive tendencies, as her risky behaviors followed her into adulthood. She was shielded from the worst of the consequences that could have resulted from her actions, however. Despite everything, she is grateful that she never got entangled in other self-destructive behaviors like drug and alcohol use. Counseling can reduce risky sexual behavior and self-destructive behaviors which may otherwise have debilitating long-term consequences over a lifetime. However, while changing behavior is an important consideration in counseling, the challenge of changing the survivor's outlook on life might be even more crucial to adjustment.

Chapter 12

LOWERED SELF-ESTEEM – A CONSEQUENCE

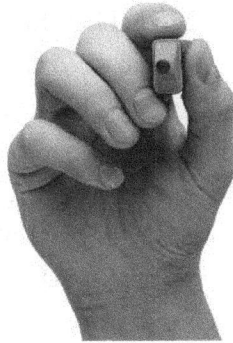

EVEN THOUGH VICTIMS of sexual assault may find social support, professional help and religious connections beneficial in their adjustment, the residual effects of this traumatic event often remain with them over a lifetime. These residual effects can be seen in social and family relationships. However, they are most clearly illustrated in the way women perceive themselves following an assault.

Perilloux, Duntley & Buss (2012) conducted a study of 49 victims of rape and 91 victims of attempted sexual assault. They confirm the results of previous studies on the statistics of the perpetrators by citing that most victims knew their perpetrators: 58.2% were friends or acquaintances; 28.4% were hopeful current or past mates; 4% were family members, and 10.4% were strangers. In this study, the researchers analyzed 13 areas in which women were potentially affected by rape: health, self-esteem, perceived attractiveness, self-perceived mate value, family relationships, work life, social life, social reputation, sexual reputation, desire to have sex, frequency of sex, enjoyment of sex, and long-term, committed relationships. Based on an analysis of these domains in combination with the victims' own accounts of their experiences, the researchers illuminated the costs of rape. They found that victims of completed rape had more negative outcomes than victims of attempted sexual assault in 11 of the 13 areas studied. The most negative outcomes were seen in areas of self-esteem, sexual reputation, frequency of sex, desire to have sex, and self-perceived mate value.

For women, the costs of rape are unbelievably enormous. "Of over 100 things a man could do to upset a woman, women rate sexually aggressive acts as the most upsetting, even more upsetting than non-sexual physical abuse and partner infidelity" (Perilloux et al, 2012, p. 1099). That however, is only a minute portion of the costs of rape according to this study. Aside from the psychological effects and unwanted pregnancies with a man who has no interest in paternal involvement, women often suffer great social effects in areas of work life, family life, sexual functioning, romantic relationships, and self-esteem. The exercise of her preferential choice of a romantic partner is taken away from her, and this leaves her with a decreased mate value. The study claims that this decreased mate value might undermine women's attempts to attract a high quality long-term mate. This experience also does damage to a woman's sexual reputation, which can lead to grave consequences for existing and future relationships. Victims of rape may have decreased value in the long-term mating market, because men prioritize cues to sexual fidelity in long-term mating, and may view rape as infidelity. If already mated, a rape victim risks losing her romantic partner who may regard her to have lowered mate value which could cause damage to his own social reputation.

According to Perilloux et al (2012), damage to a woman's reputation might serve to recalibrate her own sense of attractiveness and value. Thus, the researchers claim she settles for mates who are of substantially lower quality than she could otherwise attract. Rape can also have great negative impact on familial and social relationships. Rape of a family member can bring shame upon the family; thus, families often distance themselves from the victim to avoid society's punishment of the entire family. In addition, there are tremendous psychological costs in terms of tremendous rage, fear, self-loathing, humiliation, shame and disgust. The following are some examples of women's reports of self-perception and effects on relationships after they experienced attempted or completed rape:

"It affected my self-esteem in a negative way because I felt really dirty just like in the movies… (19 years old, attempted victimization at age 19)."

"My self-esteem plummeted after the sexual victimization. I was depressed and didn't think myself worthy of dating other guys…I just didn't have confidence in myself anymore. (23 years old, completed rape at age 18)"

"I am a Christian and past physical experiences are a big deal between Christian relationships…None of my subsequent romantic partners know about it and I do not think they would be too happy about it–they would probably blame me for it. (21 years old, attempted victimization at age 19)"

"Although I had more and more sex, I didn't like it. But my frequency went way, way, way up. I was indiscriminate because I felt that it didn't matter anymore. (22 years old, completed rape at age 19)."

"My current boyfriend is really good about it, he tries to understand and work with me, but he feels that it has more to do with him, and sometimes gets upset about it. He doesn't seem to understand how I can in my mind equate him and the other guy. I don't; it's just the situation. (20 years old, attempted victimization at age 16)."

"It ruined it. [My partner] couldn't get it out of his head that it was my fault. He started criticizing my behavior and what I wore. Basically, I think how you act and how you dress gives guys the idea that you want to have sex with them. It wasn't, "You look beautiful in that," it was, "Guys are going to think you want sex." Our relationship ended because of stuff like that. (21 years old, completed rape at age 19)."

"I realized that I may be a little more attractive than before. This actually made me begin to dress more conservatively because I was afraid of attracting someone to do this to me again. I am even now, still aware. (18 years old, attempted victimization at age 17)."

"I felt that I had to become unattractive so that it could never happen again. I didn't want to feel or be attractive. (21 years old, completed rape at age 19)."

"When I think about sex I don't think about it as a pleasure. I think about more of it as an action I will eventually have to do if I get married. (19 years old, attempted victimization at age 16)."

"Because of the traumatic experience, I remember having a fear of what would happen to my ability to enjoy sex with someone that I love… (20 years old, completed rape at age 18)."

"I seem to not enjoy sex as much because I tend to over-think the emotional vs. physical side of sex, and which one my partner is most interested in. (18 years old, attempted victimization at age 16)."

"It decreased my enjoyment of sex substantially. Every time I would have sex and manage to orgasm I immediately started feeling like a whore. It was easier if I didn't enjoy it. It was better still if I didn't have sex at all. (21 years old, completed rape at age 19)."

"I was really angry at my family for not protecting me more. (20 years old, completed rape at age 13)."

According to this study, time and the incorporation of positive life events have served to amend the costs of rape. Many of the women have either returned to normalcy or at least improved in the way they view themselves. Martha's story is a testament to the reality of this decreased self-esteem and the journey to find redemption. Over her lifetime, she subconsciously selected mates that needed saving. She seemed to have this warped idea that if she could make herself indispensable to her mate, then the relationship would last. But she was only fooling herself. All that served to do was further ruin her fragile self-esteem and make her question a lot of things about herself and her motives.

Martha's story illustrates that the path to a renewed self-perception can be a rocky one. She can identify with the women in this study regarding the negative light in which she viewed herself following the assault. As a result, she made some detours in life that caused much pain, loneliness and isolation. The lessons learned took years to assimilate, but they were necessary for her to make it to the next level. Martha does not consider herself to have arrived, as the healing process continues daily. She is ever aware of the possibility that she might fight demons for the rest of her life; but she fully intends to slay every single one.

Martha is living proof that even though mate choice may have been thwarted at a critical point in life, with the right support, a survivor of rape can go on to lead a productive and fulfilling life. At a crucial phase in her development, the choice of an ideal mate was taken from her by force. But she drew on all available resources to help her overcome the awful consequences. That was not an easy task, however. It took her being self-aware, and having a resolute determination to make the necessary adjustments to beat the odds.

Chapter 13

RESILIENCE – THE KEY

WHAT MAKES THE *difference between a person who self-destructs and one who does not?* Resilience is the key to understanding adjustment after emotional trauma. Luthar and Cicchetti (2000) define resilience as "…a dynamic process wherein individuals display positive adaptation despite experiences of significant adversity or trauma" (p. 857). They were careful to point out that this is not so much about personality. The two main concepts involved in understanding resilience are: 1) Exposure to adversity, and 2) demonstration of positive adjustment outcomes.

Adversity refers to risk, or negative life situations that have been proven to result in adjustment issues. For example, children exposed to violence or neglect usually have greater difficulty adjusting than those who are not exposed to such circumstances. These researchers define positive adjustment as social competence in terms of meeting developmental goals. In the context of resilience, positive adjustment can simply be the absence of emotional distress or behavioral problems. Depending on the type of adversity or the gravity of the situation, the absence of emotional distress might be more important than making good grades in school for example.

Ungar (2013) takes the research a little further by highlighting the importance of social services in the resilience of children exposed to adverse circumstances. He suggests that there are protective factors in the interactions between individuals and their environment that help them to adjust. These protective factors may be formal interventions from sources such as child welfare services, or special education and mental health services for example. In contrast to the previously mentioned study, Ungar views responsiveness of social services as more important than personal factors in helping children to adjust after maltreatment. His recommendation is to make support services more accessible and more flexible in responding to different types of abuse.

In a publication by The American Psychological Association (APA), resilience is defined as an ongoing process where people are required to painstakingly persevere through some deliberate steps (2017). The researchers see resilience as the factor that enables people to adapt effectively to life-changing or tragic situations and tremendously traumatic events. They claim that resilience is not as extraordinary as some are inclined to think, citing the example of the victims of the 911 terrorist attacks and their courage in rebuilding their lives. The APA concurs with other researchers who find that resilience is not a personality trait that people possess. Instead, it involves behaviors, thoughts and actions that anyone can acquire and cultivate.

According to the APA, some of the crucial factors in resilience include: 1) Having strong supportive relationships that promote love and trust, 2) having the capacity to implement effective strategies, 3) having a positive outlook and confidence in one's strengths and abilities, and 4) having the capability to handle strong feelings and impulses. They suggest making the process of building resilience a personal journey. An approach that may work for one person may not work for another. Cultural factors may play a role in the strategy one utilizes, as different cultures communicate feelings in various ways and have varying norms surrounding how they deal with hardship. The APA provides some practical ways to build resilience which may reach across cultural lines and be incorporated into your own personal strategy for developing buoyancy. Below, they are summarized into three main steps:

Seek Social Support: Making connections is the first step toward building resilience. Having positive, supportive relationships with friends or family members is extremely important. This may mean joining a religious group or a support group. There are testimonials that suggest those who help others receive certain mutual benefits themselves. Taking advantage of support systems will help victims to avoid seeing crises as insurmountable problems. While tragedy and traumatic events are oftentimes out of your control, you will not seek to control stressors, but instead, learn to respond to stressors in a more positive way. With the right support, you will also come to accept change as a part of life. Adversity can result in the loss of hopes and dreams, and make certain life goals unattainable. It is important to accept that there are some circumstances that cannot be changed. The right people around you will guide you toward focusing on those things that you have some measure of control over.

Take Decisive Action: Making steady progress toward your goals is the next step in building resilience. Goals must be realistic and achievable; but the most important thing is to make regular steps toward accomplishing these goals. These might be baby steps; but anything you do that moves you in the direction of your goal will be worthwhile. You want to face the challenges directly and be decisive in acting upon difficult situations. In this process, you must look for opportunities for self-discovery and growth as a result of adversity. With endurance and persistence, you can gain great strength in coping with hardship, and develop deeper faith and stronger relationships.

Believe in Yourself: The final step is to maintain a positive view of yourself, and trust your ability to manage strong emotions. It is important to rely on your instincts, and have confidence in yourself as you work on solving problems. Keep things in perspective as you look at the big picture. Even when the situation seems grim, it is imperative that you maintain a positive outlook and dig deep to find the strength to get to the next level. Remain optimistic about the future, and visualize what you want to happen instead of focusing on your fears. In looking beyond the present situation to a time when things will be better, you will create a reason to hope in the future.

Based on the research, it appears that both personality and environment play significant roles in a person's resilience when faced with adversity. It is evident that Mike went through some things in life; but he ended up turning to drugs instead of channeling his energies into more positive behaviors. Martha's siblings also went through their own experiences, and each took a different path in life. Grayson got into trouble with the law in Jamaica after he was deported from the States, and ended up living a very isolated life as a result. Connie became a massage therapist; but like Grayson, she also became a loner. Still, she has done very well caring for herself financially considering the circumstances. Eve fulfilled her lifelong dream and became a physician, though she would deal with many obstacles along the way. Like Martha, she possessed a certain drive to make something of her life despite the challenges.

Martha's trajectory in life demonstrates that there is a certain measure of willpower that comes into play in making it through hardships. This is manifested in help-seeking, perseverance and self-confidence. Martha had a determination that nothing would stop her from becoming fully actualized. The experiences of her childhood were constantly in her thoughts as she made her way through life. She realized that these experiences made her who she was as a person. She was always aware of how these experiences affected the decisions she made in life – whether good or bad – but refused to allow herself any excuses for failure. As such, she sought help wherever she could find it; this was among family and friends as well as clergy and professional counselors. She has persevered despite the circumstances, but she admits that she still feels a sense of isolation at times. She has developed a few close friendships, but most of her friends are married with young children. Martha's children are now grown, and on occasions that call for family time, Martha feels the brunt of that isolation. Nevertheless, she keeps herself busy with work and other meaningful service projects, and continues to believe in her ability to persevere through whatever difficulties may arise.

The main difference between the early experiences of Martha and Eve compared to that of their other siblings – Grayson and Connie – was the support Martha and Eve received from their father's relatives. Connie and Grayson did not have that other family to fall back on, as their fathers were not involved in their lives. The four years of stability that Martha and Eve had in Baker's Town was a huge factor in the way their lives turned out. Baker's Town was no *Beverly Hills,* but it was there that they formed strong family bonds with their father's relatives, and lasting friendships that would survive over time and distance. There they learned to appreciate the good times and power through the bad.

They learned to be thankful for the little they had, and to share with those in need. They learned that people are not defined by their circumstances; after all, Grandma Sutton raised 10 children in that community and not one of them ever got in trouble with the law. It was there that they learned to become strong leaders and to change the world.

The world can be unkind and downright cruel at times. However, those who exhibit the will to prevail despite adverse circumstances often come out victorious on the other side. These individuals develop effective coping skills due to their hard work and dedication to finding healing; but self-will coupled with a belief in a higher power might yield even greater rewards.

Chapter 14

Spirituality
Unlocks the Doors

A STUDY CONDUCTED at Loma Linda University Behavioral Medicine Center explored the relationship between spirituality and life's meaning among 15 individuals who were suffering from severe depression. They found four emerging themes: "(1) depression creates a sense of spiritual disconnection. Participants indicated feeling disconnected from God, the community, and oneself; (2) spirituality plays an important role in coping with the pain of depression; (3) there exists a deep yearning for a sense of meaning and a struggle to make sense of one's pain; and (4) coming to terms with one's circumstances and one's depression at some level assists in the healing process" (Sorajjakool, Aja, Chilson, Ramírez-Johnson, Earll, 2008, p. 521).

Other studies support the theory that spirituality plays a significant role in dealing with depression. In a long-term study of 114 adult offspring of depressed and non-depressed parents, researchers found a link between personal spirituality and lowered risk for depression in adults without a history of depression (Miller, Wickramaratne, Gameroff, Sage, Tenke, & Weissman, 2012). They went on to conduct 10-year and 20-year follow-up of these Catholic or Protestant individuals. They found that those who reported at the 10-year follow-up that religion or spirituality was very important to them had a 25% lower risk of major depression between year 10 and year 20 compared to other participants. According to this study, church attendance or denomination was not a significant factor in the outcome. Among those participants who had a depressed parent, the ones who reported high importance of religion had about one-tenth the risk of major depression compared to other participants.

The authors found that not only does religious affiliation protect participants against initial onset of depression, but it also protected them against recurrence. These benefits might be due to religious integrated psychotherapy often received from pastors, or engagement with clergy in times of difficulty. Clergy can offer support and help people gain perspective on their situation, and of suffering in general. In so doing clergy can help individuals to avoid potential episodes of depression.

Other studies support the theory that religiosity and spirituality offer protection against mental health issues for both social and psychological reasons (Maselko, Gilman, Buka, 2009). They define religious wellbeing in terms of the quality of one's personal relationship with God. Spirituality, on the other hand, is defined in terms of having a belief in a higher power which reflects one's sense of meaning or purpose in life. They found that individuals who reported any religious service attendance had a 30% less chance of a major depressive episode compared to those who never attend services.

It has been proven that social isolation is a major risk factor for depression. Maselko et al (2009) submit that belonging to a religious group or church community offers an opportunity for social connections. They claim that religious teachings and doctrines also provide a framework for interpreting life events, making sense of suffering, and developing a greater sense of the purpose in life. Many who have psychological health problems are often unable to make sense of life's events. Those who do not have a religious affiliation often make the statement, 'If there is a God, why is there so much suffering in life?' Thus, religious affiliation often provides that sense of a larger purpose for our sufferings.

Martha's story is an awesome illustration that connecting with God can serve to strengthen suffering individuals such that they are able to withstand trials that they never thought possible. This connection helped Martha to understand the bigger picture, though she was not able to see it during her pain and suffering. Her belief in a power outside of herself led her to accept that there are things that may never be explained in this life. It did not leave her feeling disgruntled even when there was no sign of vindication for wrongs done to her.

A spiritual connection unlocks doors of opportunities for greater things, and develops faith and resilience that can help the survivor of sexual assault to cope. The journey toward healing can be much more easily navigated when the spiritual connection is strong. This connection, provides overcoming power, frees the survivor from guilt, and essentially makes the whole experience much more manageable. Nevertheless, there are practical steps that must be taken in working through the healing process following such an ordeal.

Chapter 15
DEALING WITH THE
LOSS AND TRAUMA

ONCE AN INDIVIDUAL comes to a proper understanding of the purpose of suffering and puts things into perspective, the natural response is a desire to share the lessons learned. To avoid self-destruction and get to a place where one can give back to society, the victim of sexual assault must first focus on healing. The assault must be treated like any other traumatic event, where the victim confronts and deals with the loss – in Martha's case, the loss of hopes and dreams. One way of dealing with loss is to allow yourself time to go through the process. According to a recent publication, there are several stages a person must go through in dealing with trauma and loss: 1) Shock, denial and disbelief; 2) Anger and depression, and 3) Understanding and accepting (Aetna Resources for Living, 2016).

In the first stage, the victim might completely deny that the incident took place. The whole situation might seem surreal, and there is a certain amount of numbness as the victim seems to lose feelings. During this time, victims might try to convince themselves that the events and or consequences can be reversed. At this stage in the healing process, some days will be better than others. The good news is that the healing process has begun, so allow yourself to feel the pain. The key is to allow yourself as much time as you need, getting some extra sleep, rest and relaxation. Sticking to your daily routine will aid in the healing process as well, though this might prove to be extremely difficult.

The next stage is where the feelings start to come to the forefront. Sadness and tearfulness are not uncommon during this stage. You might even unfairly blame yourself or others around you for the circumstances. There might be angry outbursts directed at those closest to you. At this stage, you might find yourself unable to focus, unable to eat, sleep or concentrate. A sense of despair soon follows, coupled with feelings of hopelessness. It is important that you are aware of those feelings and embrace them, knowing it is part of the process. Avoid making any major decisions during this time, as you work toward acceptance of what has transpired. Connect with trusted friends or family members, and reach out to a counselor or clergy if necessary. While you are allowing yourself time to grieve the loss of your hopes and dreams, avoid stress as much as possible and engage in meaningful activities that offer a feeling of fulfilment.

Grief can be complicated, at which time, extra help is needed (Aetna Resources for Living, 2017). When grief is so intense or lasts so long that you feel your safety or the safety of someone you care about is at risk, it is time to seek professional help. Other warning signs of complicated grief include a pervasive sense of lowered self-worth, preoccupation with the loss, wishing to die, flashbacks or nightmares, self-destructive behaviors, using alcohol or drugs to avoid the pain, and difficulty managing activities of daily living. It is imperative that you seek help immediately if you have any suicidal thoughts. You may contact the National Suicide Prevention Hotline at: **800-273-8255;** however, you should call **911** if you have an emergency. Besides seeking the help of a professional, you might consider seeking out a support group and associating more frequently with friends. It is also important to take advantage of religious affiliations during this time by putting your faith to work.

The final stage is where you find peace despite the pain and suffering you endured. You find yourself letting go of what might have been and accepting what has happened. At this stage, you begin to find meaning in the situation and allow yourself to hope in the future once more. This is where you start to feel renewed strength, as you develop new coping skills.

As you find a way to forgive yourself and others who have hurt you, the pain, guilt and resentment is released and you can start putting your life back together. The crisis can be transformed into a new opportunity for you. Then, and only then, can the survivor of sexual assault begin thinking about giving back to society. Only then can one get past the psychological consequences of depression, anxiety, and low self- esteem, and avoid self-destructive behaviors which manifest in poor life choices. The survivor will begin to feel like a valuable person, worthy of love.

Individuals who have been victims of rape can come through shining as gold as Martha did. Such an experience does not have to destroy your sense of value and self-worth. It does not define who you are as a person, nor does it make you less worthy of love and affection. You are not '*damaged goods*' as some would have you believe. Instead, your experience can be transformed into creative energy and used to benefit others. It can be a tool to start a conversation with someone who might be suffering a similar plight, or to help another person to avoid falling into the same pit.

Keeping the experience to yourself can only eat away at your soul and feed the negative thoughts surrounding the event. Remaining silent can reinforce the false belief that you are to blame, or that you did something to deserve it. It can make you feel that you have something to be ashamed of, and perpetuate feelings of worthlessness. This is a trap designed to keep you in the vicious cycle of depression and anxiety. You are deserving of happiness in life, so allow yourself to accept and experience love in its purest form. *Will you ever recover all you have lost?* You must hold on to the belief that you will recapture the years that were wasted. With hard work, resilience and faith, you can be fully restored. Only then will you open yourself to the possibility of finding genuine love and acceptance in unexpected places.

References

Aetna Resources for Living (2016). Stages of Recovery from Trauma and Loss. http://promoinfotools.com/Communications/ecard/Svcs/EmPrep/StagesOfRecoveryFromTraumaAndLoss_ARFL.pdf

Aetna Resources for Living (2017). Managing Grief: How to find Joy again. https://wejoinyou.aetna.com/complicated-grief/

American Psychological Association (2017). The Road to Resilience. http://www.apa.org/helpcenter/road-resilience.aspx

Davies, M. (2002). Male sexual assault victims: A selective review of the literature and implications for support services. *Aggression and Violent Behavior, 7*(3), 203-214. Retrieved from https://www.sciencedirect.com/science/article/pii/S1359178900000434

Girelli, S. A., Resick, P. A., Marhoefer-Dvorak, S., & Hutter, C. K. (1986). Subjective distress and violence during rape: Their effects on long-term fear. *Violence and Victims, 1*(1), 35-46. Retrieved from http://search.proquest.com/docview/2085 64591?accountid=36783

Green, B. L., Krupnick, J. L., Stockton, P., Goodman, L., & et al. (2005). Effects of adolescent trauma exposure on risky behavior in college women. *Psychiatry, 68*(4), 363-78. Retrieved from http://search.proquest.com/docview/220667123?accountid=36783

Hill, T. D., Kaplan, L. M., French, M. T., & Johnson, R. J. (2010). Victimization in early life and mental health in adulthood: An examination of the mediating and moderating influences of psychosocial resources. *Journal of Health and Social Behavior, 51*(1), 48-63. Retrieved from http://search.proquest.com/docview/89200081?accountid=36783

Larsen, M. & Hilden, M. (2016). Male victims of sexual assault: 10 years' experience from a Danish assault center. *Journal of Forensic and Legal Medicine*, 43, 8-11

Luthar, S. S. & Cicchetti, D. (2000). The construct of resilience: Implications for interventions and social policies. Developmental Psychopathology, *12*(4), 857-885. https://www.ncbi.nlm.nih.gov/pmc/articles/PMC1903337/

Maselko, J., Gilman, S. E., & Buka, S. (2009). Religious service attendance and spiritual well-being are differentially associated with risk of major depression. *Psychological Medicine, 39*(6), 1009-17. doi:http://dx.doi.org/10.1017/S0033291708004418

Mezey, G. C., & King, M. B. (Eds.). (1992). *Oxford medical publications. Male victims of sexual assault.* New York, NY, US: Oxford University Press.

Miller, L., PhD, Wickramaratne, P., PhD, Gameroff, M. J., PhD, Sage, M., MA, Tenke, C. E., PhD, & Weissman, M. M., PhD. (2012). Religiosity and major depression in adults at high risk: A ten-year prospective study. *The American Journal of Psychiatry, 169*(1), 89-94. Retrieved from http://search.proquest.com/docview/1010499613?accountid=36783

Orchowski, L. M. & Gidycz, C. A. (2015). Psychological consequences associated with positive and negative responses to disclosure of sexual assault among college women: A prospective study. *Violence Against Women, 21*(7), 803–823.

Perilloux, C., Duntley, J. D., & Buss, D. M. (2012). The costs of rape. *Archives of Sexual Behavior, 41*(5), 1099-106. doi:http://dx.doi.org/10.1007/s10508-011-9863-9

Peters, D. K., & Range, L. M. (1996). Self-blame and self-destruction in women sexually abused as children. *Journal of Child Sexual Abuse, 5*(4), 19-33. Retrieved from http://search.proquest.com/docview/217513022?accountid=36783

RAINN (2018). Victims of Sexual Violence: Statistics. Retrieved from https://www.rainn.org/statistics/victims-sexual-violence

Stepakoff, S. (1998). Effects of sexual victimization on suicidal ideation and behavior in U.S. college women. *Suicide & Life - Threatening Behavior, 28*(1), 107-26. Retrieved from http://search.proquest.com/docview/224888979?accountid=36783

Ullman, S. E. & Vasquez, A. L. (2015). Mediators of sexual revictimization risk in adult sexual assault victims. *J Child Sex Abuse.; 24*(3), 300–314.

Ullman, S. E., Filipas, H. H., & Townsend, S. M. (2005). Violence and victims. *New York; 20*(4), 417-432.

Ungar, M. (2013). Resilience after maltreatment: the importance of social services as facilitators of positive adaptation. Child Abuse and Neglect, *37*(2-3), 110-115. https://www.ncbi.nlm.nih.gov/pubmed/23260114

Walker, J., Archer, J., & Davies, M. (2005). Effects of male rape on psychological functioning. *British Journal of Clinical Psychology, 44,* 445-451.

Wright, J., Friedrich, W., Cinq-Mars, C., Cyr, M., & McDuff, P. (2004). Self-destructive and delinquent behaviors of adolescent female victims of child sexual abuse: Rates and covariates in clinical and non-clinical samples. *Violence and Victims, 19*(6), 627-43. Retrieved from http://search.proquest.com/docview/208519890?accountid=36783